NEW DIRECTIONS FOR PROGRAM EVALUATION
A Publication of the American Evaluation Association

William R. Shadish, *Memphis State University*
EDITOR-IN-CHIEF

The Qualitative-Quantitative Debate: New Perspectives

Charles S. Reichardt
University of Denver

Sharon F. Rallis
Regional Laboratory for Educational Improvement of the Northeast and Islands

EDITORS

Number 61, Spring 1994

JOSSEY-BASS PUBLISHERS
San Francisco

THE QUALITATIVE-QUANTITATIVE DEBATE: NEW PERSPECTIVES
Charles S. Reichardt, Sharon F. Rallis (eds.)
New Directions for Program Evaluation, no. 61
William R. Shadish, Editor-in-Chief

Microfilm copies of issues and articles are available in 16mm and 35mm, as well as microfiche in 105mm, through University Microfilms Inc., 300 North Zeeb Road, Ann Arbor, Michigan 48106-1346.

LC 85-644749   ISSN 0164-7989   ISBN 0-7879-9967-9

NEW DIRECTIONS FOR PROGRAM EVALUATION is part of The Jossey-Bass Education Series and is published quarterly by Jossey-Bass Inc., Publishers, 350 Sansome Street, San Francisco, California 94104-1342.

Subscriptions for 1994 cost $54.00 for individuals and $75.00 for institutions, agencies, and libraries.

EDITORIAL CORRESPONDENCE should be sent to the Editor-in-Chief, William R. Shadish, Department of Psychology, Memphis State University, Memphis, Tennessee 38152.

Manufactured in the United States of America. Nearly all Jossey-Bass books, jackets, and periodicals are printed on recycled paper that contains at least 50 percent recycled waste, including 10 percent postconsumer waste. Many of our materials are also printed with vegetable-based inks; during the printing process, these inks emit fewer volatile organic compounds (VOCs) than petroleum-based inks. VOCs contribute to the formation of smog.

INSTRUCTIONS TO CONTRIBUTORS

NEW DIRECTIONS FOR PROGRAM EVALUATION (NDPE), a quarterly sourcebook, is an official publication of the American Evaluation Association. As such, NDPE publishes empirical, methodological, and theoretical work on all aspects of program evaluation and related fields. Substantive areas may include any area of social programming such as mental health, education, job training, medicine, or public health, but may also extend the boundaries of evaluation to such topics as product evaluation, personnel evaluation, policy analysis, or technology assessment. In all cases, the focus on evaluation is more important than the particular substantive topic.

NDPE does not consider or publish unsolicited single manuscripts. Each issue of NDPE is devoted to a single topic, with contributions solicited, organized, reviewed, and edited by a guest editor. Issues may take any of several forms, such as a series of related chapters, a monograph, or a long article followed by brief critical commentaries. In all cases, proposals must follow a specific format, which can be obtained from the Editor-in-Chief. These proposals are sent to members of the editorial board, and to relevant substantive experts, for peer review. This process may result in rejection, acceptance, or a recommendation to revise and resubmit. However, NDPE is committed to working constructively with potential guest editors to help them develop acceptable proposals. Close contact with the Editor-in-Chief is encouraged during proposal preparation and generation.

COPIES OF NDPE's "Guide for Proposal Development" and "Proposal Format" can be obtained from the Editor-in-Chief:

William R. Shadish, Editor-in-Chief
New Directions for Program Evaluation
Department of Psychology
Memphis State University
Memphis, Tennessee 38152
Office: 901-678-4687
FAX: 901-678-2579
Bitnet: SHADISHWR@MEMSTVX1

CONTENTS

EDITORS' NOTES

The origins of this volume can be found in the long-standing antagonism between qualitative and quantitative researchers in evaluation. This antagonism was part of the reason that the field of evaluation gave birth in the 1970s to two separate professional organizations, the Evaluation Network (ENet) and the Evaluation Research Society (ERS). When ENet and ERS decided to merge to form the American Evaluation Association (AEA) in the mid 1980s, the antagonism did not disappear, it was merely suppressed.

That these suppressed hostilities later reappeared was probably inevitable. One visible indicator that tensions were still present was an exchange among AEA presidents. It started with Yvonna Lincoln's AEA presidential address in 1990 (Lincoln, 1991). Lee Sechrest's rejoinder followed in his AEA presidential address in 1991 (Sechrest, 1992), and David Fetterman (1992), who was to become AEA president in 1993, also joined the fray. This altercation prompted David Cordray (1993), AEA president in 1992, to ask if a synthesis of the disparate views might be possible.

Providing much useful guidance and advice, David Cordray invited us to organize the plenary sessions for the 1992 AEA annual conference as a start toward answering his question about synthesis. The six speakers whom we invited all wrote papers to accompany their talks, and the present volume, *The Qualitative-Quantitative Debate: New Perspectives,* is the result.

In choosing speakers, we tried to well represent both the qualitative and quantitative perspectives. We also tried to choose speakers who, while perhaps being affiliated with one perspective more than the other, were able to converse with the other.

In Chapter One, we describe stereotypes that quantitative and qualitative researchers have of each other. Also, we show how the differences between qualitative and quantitative inquiry can be used to enrich rather than diminish evaluation practice.

In Chapter Two, Ernest R. House argues that American social science has historically overemphasized methodology to the neglect of content. He notes that neither the qualitative nor the quantitative paradigm is completely adequate as currently formulated, and that an improved integration can be achieved by focusing on both the content of evaluation and the nature of the evaluation argument.

In Chapter Three, Peter H. Rossi characterizes qualitative research as connoisseurial and quantitative research as outcome-oriented and argues that the dispute between the "quals" and "quants" is largely a struggle over market share for their different types of services. Rossi describes the historical origins of this struggle, outlines the circumstances that tend to favor one type of evaluation over the other, and calls for more truthfulness and forthrightness in advertising our different types of services.

In Chapter Four, Mary Lee Smith describes the experiences that led her to become disillusioned with quantitative methods and, correspondingly, to become attracted to qualitative methods. At the same time, she documents the problems faced by qualitative researchers, explains how these problems are often overlooked in calls for paradigmatic purity, and argues that the weaknesses in each approach can be best addressed by the use of multiple methods.

In Chapter Five, Terry E. Hedrick argues that the meaning of the terms qualitative and quantitative must be carefully defined before the relative merits of the two types of inquiry can be usefully debated. In this vein, Hedrick distinguishes among three levels of differences (paradigms, designs, and methods) and suggests that varying degrees of integration between qualitative and quantitative inquiry are possible at each of these levels. Hedrick also describes how qualitative and quantitative inquiry are often integrated at the U.S. General Accounting Office.

In Chapter Six, Lois-ellin Datta explains why the paradigm debate is surprising in its stridency and yet predictable in its timing. Datta argues that both the qualitative and quantitative paradigms have much unfinished business to which to attend and that the differences between the paradigms are far less sharp in practice than in theory. She further notes that while each paradigm has contributed much to evaluation practice, neither deserves our exclusive allegiance, and that the best is yet to come in the form of a third, more adaptive, paradigm.

In Chapter Seven, Robert K. Yin describes archetypical instances of three types of studies: qualitative, quantitative, and experimental-psychological research. Drawing on these case studies and a content analysis of research texts, Yin proposes four traits that all good research possesses and argues that these commonalities provide a shared logic that transcends the differences between qualitative and quantitative inquiry.

In Chapter Eight, we note that, in spite of the obvious differences between qualitative and quantitative inquiry, many of the arguments of epistemological incompatibility between the paradigms are incorrect, and that the two types of inquiry share many fundamental values.

After reading our contributors' chapters, we were impressed with how poorly any unidimensional categorization represents the views that are herein expressed. In this volume, the authors are not partisans defending ideological turfs but rather individuals trying to come to grips with the challenges that program evaluation faces because of a diversity of methods and practices. The focus is on the potential richness of a field that can benefit from diverse perspectives.

Charles S. Reichardt
Sharon F. Rallis
Editors

References

Cordray, D. S. "Synthesizing Evidence and Practices." *Evaluation Practice,* 1993, *14* (1), 1–8.

Fetterman, D. M. "In Response to Lee Sechrest's 1991 AEA Presidential Address: 'Roots: Back to Our First Generations,' Feb. 1991, 1–7." *Evaluation Practice,* 1992, *13,* 171–172.

Lincoln, Y. S. "The Arts and Sciences of Program Evaluation." *Evaluation Practice,* 1991, *12* (1), 1–7.

Sechrest, L. "Roots: Back to Our First Generations." *Evaluation Practice,* 1992, *13* (1), 1–7.

CHARLES S. REICHARDT is professor of psychology at the University of Denver.

SHARON F. RALLIS is coordinator of the Designing Schools for Enhanced Learning Program of the Regional Laboratory for Educational Improvement of the Northeast and Islands, Andover, Massachusetts.

Differences between the qualitative and quantitative research traditions can be used either to diminish or to enrich the practice of program evaluation.

The Relationship Between the Qualitative and Quantitative Research Traditions

Charles S. Reichardt, Sharon F. Rallis

A Quantitative Study

In 1986, Rand McNally published *Sports Places Rated: Ranking America's Best Places to Enjoy Sports* (Whittingham, 1986), which included a list of the best cities in the United States for downhill skiing (Kliewer, 1986). The number-one city on Richard Whittingham's (1986) downhill skiing list was Detroit. Also in the top ten were Akron-Canton, Buffalo, Chicago, Syracuse, Boston, and Cleveland. Of course, none of these cities is particularly well known for its skiing. In contrast, not a single city in Colorado made it onto Whittingham's top-ten list, even though Colorado enjoys a worldwide reputation for its skiing.

The reason for these surprising results is that Whittingham only ranked metropolitan areas with populations of fifty thousand or more (Kliewer, 1986). This criterion excluded all of the well-known ski resorts in Colorado. In addition, Whittingham based his rankings of metropolitan areas solely on the capacities of the ski lifts that were located within the counties that comprise the metropolitan areas. Although Denver, for example, is less than a two-hour drive from numerous ski areas, including Breckenridge, Copper Mountain, Keystone, Loveland, Winter Park, and Vail, there are no ski lifts within Denver's county boundaries, and therefore Denver was not highly ranked on the list.

In response to Whittingham's (1986) book, Kliewer (1986) interviewed Lee Morris, who is the lodge operations manager at the Riverview ski area, located a half hour from downtown Detroit. Morris reported that the ski slope at Riverview was basically an "enhanced" landfill with a 160-foot vertical rise, and that Riverview would have 2 to 12 inches of man-made snow by the following weekend. In contrast, the Keystone ski area, which is an hour and a half from downtown Denver, has a vertical rise of 2,340 feet, a ski run 3 miles long, and would have a base of 41 inches of snow that weekend. While there are four other ski areas in Detroit, all of which are larger than Riverview, John Colling of the Travel and Tourism Association of Southeast Michigan noted that "none of them are on mountains by any stretch of the imagination" (Kliewer, 1986). Colling further explained that "what we have are basically hills designed to prepare our skiers for the big slopes—the ones in the Rockies." Nonetheless, according to Whittingham's criteria, the five ski areas that lie within the Detroit metropolitan area place "it at the top of the heap," so to speak (Kliewer, 1986).

Kliewer (1986) also interviewed Whittingham, who explained that the study "couldn't take into account the quality of skiing, just the quantity." Whittingham also admitted that "they say there are lies, damn lies, and statistics. This falls into that last category, I'm afraid."

A Qualitative Study

Margaret Mead's (1928) Coming of Age in Samoa: A Psychological Study of Primitive Youth for Western Civilization is probably her most famous work and a classic in the field of anthropology (Gardner, 1993). Mead undertook the fieldwork as part of her graduate study at Columbia University. She began her research with the hypothesis that Samoan society was sexually promiscuous and, as a result, that Samoan youth were not confronted with as many stresses and strains as found in Western society. This hypothesis was chosen because it was supported by anecdotal evidence and because, if confirmed, it would have provided support for a major theoretical stance of Mead's academic mentor. While Mead's research did confirm the hypothesis, many scholars now believe that her conclusions were wrong and that she was "the gullible victim of a playful hoax" (Gardner, 1993, p. 131).

Because she did not speak the local Samoan language well, Mead conducted her interviews with the assistance of interpreters. Her most frequent interpreters were two young women, whom Mead described as her "merry companions." As Gardner (1993, p. 132) has explained, these two assistants were "embarrassed and offended by Mead's constant questions about sex," which is a "taboo topic in Samoa." Thinking that Mead was simply a curious tourist rather than a social scientist who would write about their conversations, the two assistants decided to extract revenge for their embarrassment by lying, a prank that was common in Samoan society. As a result, Mead was told whatever her assistants thought she wanted to hear. Yes, Mead was told, Samoan women were encouraged to sleep with as many men as possible before marriage, allowed to have sexual infidelities even after marriage, and moved "stress-free from childhood to adultery," so to speak (Gardner, 1993, p. 132). This information was all reported in Mead's book and generally accepted by American social scientists (not to mention American youth) for years to come.

Unfortunately, other researchers found life in Samoa to be dramatically different. Rather than a society of free love, Samoa was in fact quite constrained sexually. For example, "Female virginity was so highly prized that brides were tested for virginity before they were allowed to marry" (Gardner, 1993, p. 133). And it was also found that Samoan youth experienced the same types of difficulties in growing up as experienced by Western youth.

How Each Research Tradition Views the Other

Historically, there have been two distinguishable research traditions—the qualitative and the quantitative—in evaluation, as well as in other substantive fields such as sociology and psychology. Whittingham's (1986) study falls within the quantitative tradition, while Margaret Mead's (1928) study falls within the qualitative tradition. Adherents of each tradition often hold unflattering views of work within the other tradition. Whittingham's and Mead's studies can be used to illustrate the nature of these stereotypes.

Qualitative Critique of Quantitative Research. Whittingham's ranking of cities with ski facilities largely misses the point. It is possible that some individuals would like to know which U.S. metropolitan areas have ski lifts within their city limits. And it is certainly interesting (and, at least to us, surprising) to learn that Detroit, Akron-Canton, and the other cities on Whittingham's list have ski facilities within their county limits, even if these ski lifts are located on landfills rather than mountains. But knowing which major cities (or small resorts) are located near high-quality, mountain skiing is probably of far more interest to the typical ski buff. Certainly, Whittingham's list is irrelevant to anyone planning either a vacation or a relocation to take up skiing seriously. Yet, are not vacations or relocations the most likely reasons that people would have for buying a book that ranks America's best places to enjoy sports?

The same kind of criticism, especially by qualitative researchers, is often applied to quantitative evaluations. That is, qualitative researchers often criticize quantitative studies for their irrelevance. A researcher can carefully and reliably measure the number of ski lifts within a city's limits or a child's performance on a standardized test, but neither may be of much help either in locating high-quality skiing or in discovering what is actually being learned in an educational program. In The Little Prince, Antoine de Saint Exupéry (1943, pp. 16–17) voices the same concern (if quantitative researchers are scripted into the role of the grown-ups and qualitative researchers are scripted as the speaker): "Grown-ups love figures. When you tell them that you have made a new friend, they never ask you any questions about essential matters. They never say to you, 'What does his voice sound like? What games does he love best? Does he collect butterflies?' Instead, they demand: 'How old is he? How many brothers has he? How much does he weigh? How much money does his father make?' Only from these figures do they think they have learned anything about him." This criticism has also been attributed to Hilaire Belloc, using a somewhat less diplomatic metaphor: "Statistics are the triumph of the quantitative method, and the quantitative method is the victory of sterility and death."

Quantitative researchers might defend their work by noting that while quantitative research certainly has limitations, Whittingham's (1986) study is of unusually poor quality and should not be held up as an exemplar of the quantitative approach. Certainly, his study was not meant to be a scholarly treatise, and even he recognized its obvious shortcomings. But while conceding these particular shortcomings, qualitative researchers might be inclined to argue that the study nonetheless well characterizes the fundamental flaws of the quantitative approach, which, by their account, emphasizes numbers that misrepresent socially relevant reality.

Quantitative Critique of Qualitative Research. Margaret Mead was hoodwinked, at least partly, because her procedures lacked even the most rudimentary safeguards to protect the validity of her research. For example, in an interview with one of her interpreters years later, it was discovered that "had Mead ever pressed her two merry friends for verification of their lies, . . . they would have at once confessed, but Mead never challenged anything. She just scribbled it all down avidly in her notebooks" (Gardner, 1993, p. 134). As a result, Mead was able to confirm her preconceived notions about Samoan society without being burdened by reliable evidence. "Seek, with enough conviction aforethought, and ye shall find" (Gould, 1980, p. 164).

Quantitative researchers often suspect that qualitative research in evaluation is similarly unreliable. The unreliability may be the result of conscious lying, as in the Samoan study, or simply the result of respondents' unconscious bias and self-interest. That is, respondents can be telling the truth as they see it and still be quite wrong about what is really going on. Quantitative researchers also suspect that qualitative evaluators often are merely confirming preconceived notions and are blind to plausible alternative explanations.

In anthropological fieldwork, getting so caught up in the culture under study that the researcher loses his or her perspective or shifts his or her focus from research to other matters is called "going native." For example, Margaret Mead is thought to have had a sexual affair with a Samoan, which, among other things, made her assistants less hesitant in conducting their hoax (Gardner, 1993). In evaluation, perhaps the equivalent of going native in anthropological fieldwork is becoming an advocate for the positions espoused by the respondents with whom one feels most sympathy. This advocacy is also a common criticism of qualitative research in evaluation.

In their defense, qualitative researchers might note that while qualitative research does have limitations, Margaret Mead's study was unusually problematic and that much has been done to improve the use of qualitative methods since the 1920s. For example, qualitative researchers are well aware of the potential influence of preconceived ideas and have spent considerable energy developing safeguards to ensure the integrity of their research (Kirk and Miller, 1986; Lincoln and Guba, 1986). But quantitative researchers might be inclined to respond that the fundamental flaws of qualitative research are no less real simply because they were exaggerated in Margaret Mead's study.

Where Does This Leave Us? Given these characterizations that researchers within each tradition offer about the other, it is not surprising that suspicions and antagonisms rage between the two camps. Each tradition views the other negatively, perhaps even as fatally flawed. In turn, each tradition feels unfairly criticized by the other. In other words, each tradition believes that its criticisms of the other are accurate and that the criticisms by the other are overblown. The resulting animosity has developed into a long-running feud.

But though the animosity may be understandable, the way in which this conflict between the two traditions continues to be played out is not particularly healthy or beneficial for anyone, except perhaps the opponents of program evaluation. We need to find ways to improve the relationship between the two traditions so that we are enriched by our diversity more and diminished by it less.

Recognizing One's Own Weaknesses

A critique of one's work by another can be of great value. This is because it is often not easy to recognize one's own flaws and limitations. For example, one is often less aware of the limitations of one's own actions than is another person such as a spouse, a psychotherapist, a member of the loyal opposition in politics, an opponent in sports, or a manuscript reviewer in publishing. The qualitative and quantitative research traditions can provide, for each other, the alternative perspective needed to recognize and appreciate one's own weaknesses.

Of course, in helping each other recognize weaknesses, our insights and critiques will be most useful if offered in a constructive fashion. To have the flaws in one's work pointed out in an arrogant, belittling, and vicious manner, as is often done in the debates between qualitative and quantitative researchers, is infuriating, especially when the person criticizing is far from flawless.

In addition, the antagonistic critiques of each camp by the other suffer from stereotypes of two different kinds. First, each tradition tends to exaggerate the flaws in the other tradition, just as Whittingham's and Mead's studies are exaggerations. In fact, quantitative studies typically are not focused on irrelevant topics, and qualitative studies typically are not unreliable. Being a quantitative researcher does not mean that one is heartless, and being a qualitative researcher does not mean that one is soft-headed (Sechrest, 1992).

Second, each tradition tends to underestimate its own flaws. Indeed, each tradition often suffers from much the same flaws that it finds in the other tradition. For example, while they may smirk at the lies told to Margaret Mead by her informants, quantitative researchers need to be concerned that their own respondents do not lie on questionnaires and tests. Moreover, although Mead's preconceptions led her to find what she was looking for, fishing through data also allows plenty of room for preconceived notions to operate in quantitative research. Conversely, qualitative researchers criticize quantitative researchers for their lack of relevance, yet they often fail to focus their own studies on indicators of program effects other than those based on the perceptions of the participants. For example, a qualitative study is irrelevant to the extent that it ignores the effects that laetrile actually has on cancer and focuses only on the effects that consumers believe it has. Neither tradition has found the holy grail of research methods, which makes a "holier-than-thou" attitude unjustified.

Overcoming One's Own Weaknesses

To the extent their limitations differ, two methods can be better than one. This advantage was demonstrated in a collaborative study by Goldring and Rallis (1993). Based on Rallis's qualitative case studies from an evaluation of school change, an image of a new type of school emerged, one that successfully embraced change programs. While the descriptions of the schools were rich in detail, Rallis's qualitative studies had no way of demonstrating that this kind of school existed in appreciable numbers. Was the phenomenon widespread or was this the full extent? This question could be answered because Goldring had conducted several analyses of the massive data set in High School and Beyond: Administration and Teacher Survey (U.S. Department of Education, 1984) and had discovered that the pattern was indeed widespread. By combining the results from their separate studies, they were able to present a richer and more useful conceptualization of a "dynamic school" (Goldring and Rallis, 1993).

The qualitative and quantitative research traditions can also inform each other in ways that go beyond the combination of research methods. For example, a voluminous and fascinating literature on social cognition has been produced within the quantitative tradition (Gilovich, 1991). The insights that this research offers on how people cope with uncertainty and the conditions under which they consistently miscomprehend reality might well be relevant to qualitative researchers interested in understanding a participant's construction of a social program. Conversely, the narrative style of the qualitative tradition, which is usually more readable and comprehendible than the technical reports of the quantitative tradition, can reveal ways to make the work of quantitative researchers more interesting and influential.

Conclusion

The qualitative and quantitative research traditions differ. Qualitative researchers usually seek to explicate the meaning of social reality from the participants' perspectives, while quantitative researchers usually seek to understand relationships, often of a causal nature, without particular emphasis on the participants' perspectives. Nonetheless, at the most global level, the two traditions have a common goal: to understand and improve the human condition.

A defensible understanding of reality can withstand scrutiny from different perspectives and methodologies. Indeed, given its complexities and multiple facets, a complete understanding of human nature is likely to require more than one perspective and methodology. The qualitative and quantitative traditions can provide a binocular vision with which to deepen our understandings. That the qualitative and quantitative perspectives remain partly adversarial in their relationship does not preclude cooperation in working together toward their shared goal. In fact, just the opposite is true. By working together, the two traditions can enhance the practice and utilization of research and evaluation.

References

Gardner, M. "The Great Samoan Hoax." Skeptical Inquirer, 1993, 17 (2), 131–135.

Gilovich, T. How We Know What Isn't So: The Fallibility of Human Reason in Everyday Life. New York: Free Press, 1991.

Goldring, E. B., and Rallis, S. F. Principals of Dynamic Schools. Newbury Park, Calif.: Sage, 1993.

Gould, S. J. The Panda's Thumb: More Reflections in Natural History. New York: Norton, 1980.

Kirk, J., and Miller, M. L. Reliability and Validity in Qualitative Research. Newbury Park, Calif.: Sage, 1986.

Kliewer, T. D. "America's Top Skiing Mecca? Why, Detroit!" Denver Post, Dec. 12, 1986, p. 1A.

Lincoln, Y. S., and Guba, E. G. "But Is It Rigorous? Trustworthiness and Authenticity in Naturalistic Evaluation." In D. D. Williams (ed.), Naturalistic Evaluation. New Directions for Program Evaluation, no. 30. San Francisco: Jossey-Bass, 1986.

Mead, M. Coming of Age in Samoa: A Psychological Study of Primitive Youth for Western Civilization. New York: Morrow, 1928.

Saint Exupéry, A. de. The Little Prince. (K. Woods, trans.) Orlando, Fla.: Harcourt Brace Jovanovich, 1943.

Sechrest, L. "Roots: Back to Our First Generations." Evaluation Practice, 1992, 13 (1), 1–7.

U.S. Department of Education. High School and Beyond: Administration and Teacher Survey. Washington, D.C.: Government Printing Office, 1984.

Whittingham, R. Sports Places Rated: Ranking America's Best Places to Enjoy Sports. Skokie, Ill.: Rand McNally, 1986.

CHARLES S. REICHARDT is professor of psychology at the University of Denver.

SHARON F. RALLIS is coordinator of the Designing Schools for Enhanced Learning Program of the Regional Laboratory for Educational Improvement of the Northeast and Islands, Andover, Massachusetts.

One way of resolving the quantitative versus qualitative methods dispute is to recognize that evaluation has a special content and that this content is more important than the methodologies.

Integrating the Quantitative and Qualitative

Ernest R. House

Evaluation has now reached a certain maturity. The field has established itself as a worthwhile profession, valuable for what it can contribute to modern societies. I expect its role, activities, and influence to be much greater in the next fifty years. Furthermore, evaluation has become a discipline, two essential features of which are forums for critical debates within the field and an elaborated conceptual structure in which key issues can be "joined," fitted together in such a way that they can be debated productively. Scholars do not have to agree on issues, but they must be able to discuss them extensively in their disagreements. Otherwise, it is not possible for the disciplinary discourse to progress (House, 1993).

One particularly contentious issue has been the dispute over quantitative and qualitative methods. If we have a discipline, we should be able to debate this issue productively. I do not expect such debates to be unemotional, only that they be reasoned, so that progress can be made. Certainly, there is a long history to this dispute, going back many decades (J. Smith, 1983; Bannister, 1987; Hammersley, 1989; Ross, 1991). What prospects are there for resolution?

In this chapter, I argue that methodology depends primarily on the subject matter of what is investigated, and on certain background assumptions. Debates about methodology are productive only if the subject matter is considered first. In evaluation, this subject matter is the determination of the merit or worth of something. Findings from quantitative and qualitative methods

I thank Anne Colgan, Margaret Eisenhart, Ken Howe, Bob Linn, Felix Rasco, Sharon Rallis, and Charles Reichardt for helpful comments.

come together in the content of what is said, which is represented in the narrative of the study. Content is most important. Historically, methodology has been greatly overemphasized, at the expense of content. Obsession with the quantitative-qualitative dispute indicates a continued fixation on methods. Methods are important, but they should play a facilitative role. Hence, the quantitative-qualitative dispute is dated and directs attention away from important issues.

Subject Matter of Evaluation

Research methodology depends primarily on the nature of the subject matter of the discipline, the content, the object of what one is trying to investigate. In astronomy, for example, it is rather difficult to do intervention experiments. The subject matter precludes it. On the other hand, the subject matter does lend itself to precise prediction. As the content under investigation changes, as black holes are discovered, for example, the methods of investigation may also change: New methods may be needed to deal with reformulated content.

What is the subject matter of evaluation? What is there to find out? What there is to find out is how good something is. Evaluation is the determination of the merit or worth of something, according to a set of criteria, with those criteria (often but not always) explicated and justified. Scriven (1980) has provided the basic logic: X is good, bad, better than Y, and so on, in the following way, according to these criteria along these dimensions, for these reasons. This statement and its variations are the core logic of the discipline, regardless of what approach one employs. Of course, such statements can be difficult to construct and complex in their embodiments. How to arrive at justifiable evaluative judgments is the knowledge and craft of the field.

Also, evaluations are constructed and presented as arguments, and these arguments can vary significantly, including those that feature quantitative or qualitative data (House, 1977; Dunn, 1982). Evaluators, like scientists, use facts, numbers, logic, stories, and metaphors (the latter often construed as models) to construct their arguments (House, 1983; McCloskey, 1990). The arguments vary in part according to the audiences to whom they are addressed, so that evaluative argument is not only about a subject matter but also for particular audiences.

There is an analytical distinction between the form of the argument and the content, which in evaluation is a complex version of "X is good, bad, in this way." There is a content to be conveyed, a real-world condition to be determined, even though the methods of determination, the statement of the condition, and the arguments may differ. There is a content to evaluation that is no more arbitrary than that in other disciplines. To say something is good is no more arbitrary than to say something is big, although it may be more difficult to defend. An elephant is big compared to other animals (usually the implicit comparison) but small compared to an office building. Establishing evaluative judgments requires defining the context of the judgment, as well as the dimensions of merit and standards of performance, though often the context is assumed or implicit.

Of course, these judgments often involve multidimensional criteria and conflicting interests. For example, the judgment "The Reagan economic policies were very good for the upper 1 percent of the population but very bad for the bottom 10 percent" is probably defensible, but it requires considerable work to justify. One would have to show not only that the bottom 10 percent did not do well economically but also that the gains of the top 1 percent did not help the bottom 10 percent in the long run. Programs and policies can be good or bad simultaneously, when different criteria, perspectives, points of view, interests, and time frames are taken into consideration. But this amounts to refinement and elaboration of evaluative reasoning, not its abnegation.

The things that we evaluate also differ in content. Policies are not the same as products, and neither is the same as persons or programs. Evaluation of economic policies addresses different content from evaluation of television sets. Different expertise is required, and probably different methods as well. In program evaluation, exactly how one conceives and defines a program makes a difference. Matters of content make a difference in which methods should be employed. Nonetheless, the basic evaluative reasoning holds.

What also holds is that the evaluator should strive to reduce biases in making such judgments. Some bias reduction techniques are the same for both quantitative and qualitative approaches, but other techniques differ. Quantitative evaluators must be especially careful with sampling and statistics, since so much depends on them. Similarly, qualitative evaluators must be careful with interviews and narratives. On the other hand, quantitative evaluators cannot totally neglect the narratives of their studies, any more than qualitative evaluators can afford to be oblivious as to whom they interview.

Underlying Assumptions

Methodology also depends on ontological and epistemological assumptions about the nature of reality and the best ways of gaining access to that reality, so that knowledge about it can be formulated. These background assumptions provide a framework, much of it implicit, for making methodological choices (Shadish, Cook, and Leviton, 1991). There are choices about exactly what to investigate, how open-ended the study should be, how important the views of participants are, how to collect, analyze, and interpret data, what arguments to employ, and how to present results. (Of course, most of us employ the methodology we learned in graduate school, not aware of the assumptions and history behind it.)

The quantitative-qualitative dispute has been most strongly registered by some as an irreconcilable conflict between the assumptions of the positivist and interpretivist paradigms (Guba and Lincoln, 1989). An interpretivist summarized the differences this way: "One approach takes a subject-object position on the relationship to subject matter; the other takes a subject-subject position. One separates facts and values, while the other perceives them as inextricably mixed. One searches for laws, and the other seeks understanding. These positions do not seem to be compatible given our present state of thinking" (J. Smith, 1983, p. 12). These differences play out as dichotomies of objectivity versus subjectivity, fixed versus emergent categories, outsider versus insider perspectives, facts versus values, explanation versus understanding, and single versus multiple realities. Conceived in this way, the two approaches are not compatible.

However, neither of these so-called paradigms is fully adequate. The positivist tradition is correct to stress that there are causal tendencies at work in social life and to insist that these tendencies may be opaque in relation to the agents' spontaneous understanding. Where it errs is in the reduction of these tendencies to empirical regularities and in the account it gives of how to discover them (Bhaskar, 1979). The view that scientific inferences involve no extratheoretical or extraobservational judgments, but are facts methodically inferred about an uninterpreted reality, is not correct.

The interpretivist tradition, on the other hand, is correct to point out that the social sciences deal with a preinterpreted reality that is already understood through the concepts of intentional social actors, through material similar to that in which researchers will grasp it. Where it errs is in reducing knowledge to just the modalities of this relationship, as if there were nothing more (Bhaskar, 1979). It neglects external causes and conditions, unintended consequences, and the internal contradictions of social beliefs, rules, and actions (Howe, 1985, 1992).

The dichotomy between these two traditions rests on a misunderstanding of science (Toulmin, 1982). One must take account of both the beliefs and rules of participants and the causes of social practices. There must be both insider and outsider perspectives. A better set of assumptions includes the following: (1) The real world is complex and stratified, so that one is always discovering more complex layers of reality to explain other layers. (2) Society does not exist outside of individual actions; rather, social actors produce and reproduce social structures, consciously and unconsciously, which influence their actions in turn. (3) Human action is intentional, including a capacity for monitoring and second-order monitoring (the monitoring of monitoring, that is, evaluation). (4) There are no incorrigible foundations for science, such as sense impressions or pristine facts. Rather, knowledge is social and historical. (5) Scientific explanation is explanation of how causal structures of different kinds produce events. (6) The regularity theory of causation based on assumptions of invariant regularities is incorrect. (7) Social science knowledge depends on an understanding of the meaningful social world of participants. (8) There is no rigid fact-value distinction: Value claims can be established in ways similar to factual claims.

Integration of Methods

The investigation of such a complex social reality sometimes leads to the use of multiple research methods, of which the quantitative and qualitative constitute entire families (Fetterman, 1988). Quantitative studies are more precise, explicit, and predetermined and assume that the relevant variables can be identified in advance and validly measured. They direct attention to variables of interest, reduce distractions, permit fine discriminations, and facilitate concise analysis and management of data (Howe, 1985, 1988). They use mathematical models as simplified representations of substantive problems, so that results depend not only on proper analysis but also on the fit between the model and problem (House, 1977; Trochim, 1986; see Cordray, 1986, for an example).

Qualitative studies rely on more provisional questions, data collection sites, people to interview, and things to observe. They assume less in advance, including which variables are relevant, and are more open-ended, sensitive to context, and likely to be focused on the intentions, explanations, and judgments of participants (Howe, 1985). In sociology, for example, Giddens (1984) has said that qualitative methods help elucidate the frames of meaning of the actors and investigate the context of action, while quantitative methods help identify the bounds of knowledgeability of the actors and specify the institutional order, the more structural aspects of social life.

Nonetheless, even though the methods are distinct, the findings from them blend into one another in the content. When examined closely, quantitative data turn out to be composites of qualitative interpretations, though these may be hidden by extensive data processing (Giddens, 1984). According to Campbell (1974), qualitative knowledge of the local context is necessary for generating plausible alternative explanations, describing the program, constructing a narrative history, presenting data collection procedures, and summarizing results, even in quantitative studies. As Reichardt and Cook (1979, p. 23) observed, "Quite simply, researchers cannot benefit from the use of numbers if they do not know, in common sense terms, what the numbers mean."

Furthermore, at the level of inference, any conceptual theory, scheme, or hypothesis presupposes substantive qualitative beliefs that play an inescapable role in drawing conclusions (Howe, 1985). Inferences depend on substantive relationships. If one examines the content of any particular evaluation, only a portion of it will be derived from the methods. All approaches rely heavily on common sense, prior experience, and the logic of the situation (Huberman, 1987).

For example, consider an evaluation of a reading program in which mixed methods are used. Standardized test scores are collected in a randomized, control group design, and students are interviewed after the program as to what they have learned. Suppose the test score comparison indicates that there is no learning gain, but the interviews indicate that the new-program students have a deeper understanding of the subject matter. Does the evaluator say, "Well, quantitatively the program is a failure, but qualitatively, it was successful"? Or

"The program is a failure in the quantitative worldview, but a success in the qualitative worldview"? This hardly seems satisfactory.

Rather, the evaluator will search for reasons for the discrepancy. Did the test measure the deeper understandings? Were the interviews biased because of the way in which the questions were presented, analyzed, or interpreted? Were different criteria used? The evaluator would invoke basic evaluative reasoning and relevant content to reconcile the conflicting findings. The findings would be integrated to produce an overall conclusion (which does not mean that they would converge necessarily). A serious discrepancy requires justification.

How is it possible for these things to blend together? The findings from whatever methods come together in the content, which is presented as an argument, a narrative, or even a story. Kidder and Fine (1987, p. 69) contended that "all research is a form of story telling, some more obvious than others. Randomized experiments are the least obvious. . . . Nonetheless, beneath the technical language is a story about how people behave under various conditions." Stories have at least three events joined in such a way that the first precedes the second in time, the second precedes the third, and the second causes the third (McCloskey, 1990): "John was poor, won the lottery, and became rich." Compare this to "The treatment causes the effect for persons (or units) X in condition Y," which is the generic causal statement of validity typologies (Mark, 1986, p. 50).

Furthermore, the particular arguments, narratives, and stories of evaluators must concern good and bad, and they must be true. Of course, we do not call our studies stories, given the unreliability that this term suggests. Rather, we call them experiments or plausible interpretations or case studies. I believe that they are in fact arguments, even when they are in story form. In any case, the content is presented in the narrative, with narrative styles varying from the scientific to the literary. And when we simply present numbers or other uninterpreted data, such as test scores, audiences provide their own narratives as to what the data mean.

There is a further question as to whether employing different methods leads an evaluator to different findings. For example, the qualitative evaluator will assemble interview data, which contain content that a set of test scores does not, and vice versa. The evaluators will have arrived at different information to which they are led by their respective approaches. On the other hand, this information must be analyzed and interpreted within the logic of evaluation as to whether the program is good or bad, and the findings should fit together, unless the evaluators have used different criteria of merit.

Within the logic of evaluation, if evaluators use different criteria, they will arrive at different conclusions. Do different methods lead evaluators to different criteria? I am inclined to say yes, in the sense that those who want to emphasize criteria derived from participants will more likely employ qualitative techniques. However, this is a difference in the formulation and content of the evaluation and should be discussed according to whether participant criteria should be employed, not submerged in differences in methods. Methodology is the wrong focus. Where interactions between content and method do obtain, that argues for multiple, complementary methods, not for the existence of multiple realities.

Clearly, I do not believe that quantitative and qualitative methods represent distinct paradigms that incorporate incommensurate worldviews. Qualitative methods have opened new areas of content, but this content is part of the same world. Without elaborating, let me state the accepted philosophical position on incommensurability: "The dominant metaphor of conceptual relativism, that of differing points of view, seems to betray an underlying paradox. Different points of view make sense only if there is a common coordinate system on which to plot them; yet the dominant coordinate system belies the claim of dramatic incomparability" (Davidson, 1982, p. 67).

There is also the important practical problem of how to combine methods in studies. Reichardt and Cook (1979) contended that a combination of methods strengthens individual studies, and M. Smith (1986) delineated circumstances in which the combining of methods is particularly appropriate. Light and Pillemer (1984) suggested specific ways of combining such results in literature reviews, and Greene, Caracelli, and Graham (1989) studied features of mixed-method studies. Robert Linn (personal communication) suggested that quantitative and qualitative methods could be related to each other iteratively, with the researcher going back and forth, progressively clarifying the findings of one with those of the other. We need more good examples (for example, Smith, Gabriel, Schott, and Padia, 1976; M. Smith, 1986; Trend, 1979; Maxwell, Bashook, and Sandlow, 1986). We are restricted here only by our ingenuity and resources, although there are significant limitations to multiple-method studies (Mark and Shotland, 1987; Shotland and Mark, 1987). They are not panaceas.

So, in evaluation, the findings of quantitative and qualitative methods are integratable at the level of content. In the social sciences, findings from different methods are integratable at the level of theory, with each social science having its own methods of investigation (Howe and Eisenhart, 1990). Hence, the choice does not have to be between a mechanistic science or an intentionalist humanism, but rather one of conceiving science as the social activity that it is, an activity that involves considerable judgment, regardless of the methods employed. Even the natural sciences are critical interpretations of their subject matter, but this does not mean that they cannot be rational and objective (Toulmin, 1982).

Paradigm Wars

Finally, how can we account for our own actions in the "paradigm wars"? As with all wars, there is a history. Early in their development, the American social sciences shied away from certain issues of content because of strong political, social, and ideological pressures (Ross, 1991). Instead, they focused on methodology as the way to value-free, politics-free, and trouble-free findings that were consistent with an implacable belief in American exceptionality, the idea that America was so special it would not have the same social problems as other countries. This position gave rise to a virulent scientism, a fixation on methods as the center of social research (Bannister, 1987).

Science was conceived as the employment of certain methods and procedures, a methodological activity, rather than an intellectual, communal one. When particular methods were revealed as inadequate, which they always were, the reaction was to invent new methods. The result was a turning away from issues of content (and value) to an overemphasis on methodology. Chomsky (1977, p. 46) captured this turn by calling behaviorist psychology a methodology without a subject matter: "Many people think of psychology in terms of its tests and experimental methods. But one should not define a discipline by its procedures. It should be defined, in the first place, by the object of its investigation. Experimental or analytic procedures must be devised in order to shed light on this object. Behaviorist psychology, for example, excels in its experimental techniques, but it has not properly defined its object of inquiry, in my opinion. Thus it has excellent tools, very good tools . . . but nothing very much to study with them." This misplaced emphasis on method carried over to the new field of evaluation. Thirty years ago, quantitative methods alone were deemed sufficiently objective for evaluation.

The reaction to the mistakes and excesses of positivism was interpretivism, with its own excesses. Overemphasis on method led to definition by opposition: If one method was quantitative, the other was qualitative; if one was objective, the other was subjective (Guba and Lincoln, 1989). This schism was reinforced by strong emotion: The difficulty of establishing the legitimacy of qualitative methods in the face of formidable resistance increased the stridency with which they were advanced (Lincoln, 1990, 1991; Sechrest, 1992). Like any group that feels suppressed, qualitativists advocated their position passionately and often in excess.

Historically, the legitimacy of qualitative approaches was secured by distinguishing between the two approaches—attacking the quantitative and defending the qualitative. The success of this strategy makes it more difficult to abandon the dispute now that qualitative methods are legitimate. On the other side, some quantitative evaluators have been somewhat disingenuous in pretending that the establishment of qualitative methods was anything other than a long, hard-fought struggle.

Now there are those who believe that qualitative methods are the way to the promised land. Some believe that qualitative methodology will lead to a new world of promise and joy. This is the same millennial hope transferred to new methodologies, reaffirming the long-standing belief in the transformative powers of methodology. Our obsession with the quantitative-qualitative dispute reflects our continued fixation on method. In fact, all research methods are everyday work tools, likely to get our hands dirty. Methodology is important, but it is no substitute for content. There is no guaranteed methodological path to the promised land. There is nothing mystical or transformative about methods of any kind. We can kiss a frog if we want, hoping that it will turn into a handsome prince; but when we open our eyes, we will still find a frog.

References

Bannister, R. C. Sociology and Scientism: The American Quest for Objectivity, 1880–1940. Berkeley and Los Angeles: University of California Press, 1987.

Bhaskar, R. The Possibility of Naturalism. Atlantic Highlands, N.J.: Humanities Press, 1979.

Campbell, D. T. "Qualitative Knowing in Action Research." Kurt Lewin Award address presented at the annual meeting of the American Psychological Association, New Orleans, La., Sept. 1974.

Chomsky, N. Language and Responsibility. New York: Pantheon, 1977.

Cordray, D. S. "Quasi-Experimental Analysis: A Mixture of Methods and Judgment." In W.M.K. Trochim (ed.), Advances in Quasi-Experimental Design and Analysis. New Directions for Program Evaluation, no. 31. San Francisco: Jossey-Bass, 1986.

Davidson, D. "On the Very Idea of a Conceptual Scheme." In M. Krausz and J. W. Meiland (eds.), Relativism: Cognitive and Moral. South Bend, Ind.: University of Notre Dame Press, 1982.

Dunn, W. N. "Reforms as Arguments." In E. R. House, S. Mathison, J. Pearsol, and H. Preskill (eds.), Evaluation Studies Review Annual. Vol. 7. Newbury Park, Calif.: Sage, 1982.

Fetterman, D. M. "Qualitative Approaches to Evaluating Education." Educational Researcher, 1988, 17 (8), 17–22.

Giddens, A. The Constitution of Society. Berkeley and Los Angeles: University of California Press, 1984.

Greene, J. C., Caracelli, V. J., and Graham, W. F. "Toward a Conceptual Framework for Mixed-Method Evaluation Designs." Educational Evaluation and Policy Analysis, 1989, 11 (3), 255–274.

Guba, E. G., and Lincoln, Y. S. Fourth-Generation Evaluation. Newbury Park, Calif.: Sage, 1989.

Hammersley, M. The Dilemma of Qualitative Method: Herbert Blumer and the Chicago Tradition. London: Routledge & Kegan Paul, 1989.

House, E. R. The Logic of Evaluative Argument. Los Angeles: Center for the Study of Evaluation, University of California, 1977.

House, E. R. "How We Think About Evaluation." In E. R. House (ed.), Philosophy of Evaluation. New Directions for Program Evaluation, no. 19. San Francisco: Jossey-Bass, 1983.

House, E. R. Professional Evaluation: Social Impact and Political Consequences. Newbury Park, Calif.: Sage, 1993.

Howe, K. R. "Two Dogmas of Educational Research." Educational Researcher, 1985, 14 (8), 10–18.

Howe, K. R. "Against the Quantitative-Qualitative Incompatibility Thesis, or Dogmas Die Hard." Educational Researcher, 1988, 17 (8), 10–16.

Howe, K. R. "Getting Over the Quantitative-Qualitative Debate." American Journal of Education, 1992, 100 (2), 236–256.

Howe, K. R., and Eisenhart, M. "Standards for Qualitative (and Quantitative) Research: A Prolegomenon." Educational Researcher, 1990, 19 (4), 2–9.

Huberman, A. M. "How Well Does Educational Research Really Travel?" Educational Researcher, 1987, 16 (1), 5–13.

Kidder, L. H., and Fine, M. "Qualitative and Quantitative Methods: When Stories Converge." In M. M. Mark and R. L. Shotland (eds.), Multiple Methods in Program Evaluation. New Directions for Program Evaluation, no. 35. San Francisco: Jossey-Bass, 1987.

Light, R. J., and Pillemer, D. B. Summing Up: The Science of Reviewing Research. Cambridge, Mass.: Harvard University Press, 1984.

Lincoln, Y. S. "The Making of a Constructivist: A Remembrance of Transformations Past." In E. G. Guba (ed.), The Paradigm Dialog. Newbury Park, Calif.: Sage, 1990.

Lincoln, Y. S. "The Arts and Sciences of Program Evaluation." Evaluation Practice, 1991, 12 (1), 1–7.

McCloskey, D. N. If You're So Smart: The Narrative of Economic Expertise. Chicago: University of Chicago Press, 1990.

Mark, M. M. "Validity Typologies and the Logic and Practice of Quasi-Experimentation." In W.M.K. Trochim (ed.), Advances in Quasi-Experimental Design and Analysis. New Directions for Program Evaluation, no. 31. San Francisco: Jossey-Bass, 1986.

Mark, M. M., and Shotland, R. L. "Alternative Models for the Use of Multiple Methods." In M. M. Mark and R. L. Shotland (eds.), Multiple Methods in Program Evaluation. New Directions for Program Evaluation, no. 35. San Francisco: Jossey-Bass, 1987.

Maxwell, J. A., Bashook, J. A., and Sandlow, R. "Combining Ethnographic and Experimental Methods in Educational Evaluation: A Case Study." In D. M. Fetterman and M. A. Pittman (eds.), Educational Evaluation: Ethnography in Theory, Practice, and Politics. Newbury Park, Calif.: Sage, 1986.

Reichardt, C. S., and Cook, T. D. "Beyond Qualitative Versus Quantitative Methods." In T. D. Cook and C. S. Reichardt (eds.), Qualitative and Quantitative Methods in Evaluation Research. Newbury Park, Calif.: Sage, 1979.

Ross, D. The Origins of American Social Science. New York: Cambridge University Press, 1991.

Scriven, M. The Logic of Evaluation. Point Reyes, Calif.: Edgepress, 1980.

Sechrest, L. "Roots: Back to Our First Generation." Evaluation Practice, 1992, 13 (1), 1–7.

Shadish, W. R., Jr., Cook, T. D., and Leviton, L. C. Foundations of Program Evaluation: Theories of Practice. Newbury Park, Calif.: Sage, 1991.

Shotland, R. L., and Mark, M. M. "Improving Inferences from Multiple Methods." In M. M. Mark and R. L. Shotland (eds.), Multiple Methods in Program Evaluation. New Directions for Program Evaluation, no. 35. San Francisco: Jossey-Bass, 1987.

Smith, J. K. "Quantitative Versus Qualitative Research: An Attempt to Clarify the Issue." Educational Researcher, 1983, 12 (3), 6–13.

Smith, M. L. "The Whole Is Greater: Combining Qualitative and Quantitative Evaluation Approaches in Evaluation Studies." In D. D. Williams (ed.), Naturalistic Evaluation. New Directions for Program Evaluation, no. 30. San Francisco: Jossey-Bass, 1986.

Smith, M. L., Gabriel, R., Schott, J., and Padia, W. L. "Evaluation of the Effects of Outward Bound." In G. V. Glass (ed.), Evaluation Studies Review Annual. Vol. 1. Newbury Park, Calif.: Sage, 1976.

Toulmin, S. "The Construal of Reality: Criticism in Modern and Postmodern Science." Critical Inquiry, 1982, 9 (1), 93–111.

Trend, M. G. "On the Reconciliation of Qualitative and Quantitative Analyses: A Case Study." In T. D. Cook and C. S. Reichardt (eds.), Qualitative and Quantitative Methods in Evaluation Research. Newbury Park, Calif.: Sage, 1979.

Trochim, W.M.K. "Editor's Notes." In W.M.K. Trochim (ed.), Advances in Quasi-Experimental Design and Analysis. New Directions for Program Evaluation, no. 31. San Francisco: Jossey-Bass, 1986.

ERNEST R. HOUSE is professor of education at the University of Colorado, Boulder.

The historical roots and current sources of the conflict between quanti-
tative and qualitative evaluation styles is explored in this chapter, and
a proposal for reconciliation is advanced that marks out separate turfs
for the contending parties.

The War Between the Quals and the Quants: Is a Lasting Peace Possible?

Peter H. Rossi

The aphorism "Blessed be the peacemakers!" is often a call for open season on would-be conciliators. Despite the risks, I attempt in this chapter to lay out some terms for an armistice that has a chance of leading to a lasting peace. The war in question is the sometimes rancorous dispute between the advocates of quantitative versus qualitative approaches to evaluation, the "quants" and "quals."

In the spirit of full disclosure, I need to inform the reader about myself and my perspective on evaluation. First, I am a card-carrying sociologist, a minority discipline in the American Evaluation Association (AEA). Shadish, Cook, and Leviton (1991) billed me as an evaluation theorist, but that is not the label I give myself. I consider myself primarily an *evaluation researcher,* having practiced that craft for almost all of my professional life. My work classifies me as a quant, with a specialization in sample surveys. The sample survey is not the only research tool I have used: I have also conducted a large-scale field experiment and several qualitative studies.

Besides writings on evaluation, including what I hope is a widely used introductory textbook (Rossi and Freeman, 1993), most of my professional activities over the last four decades have been heavily concerned with the social problems facing American society—educational opportunity, inequality and social mobility, civil disorders, natural disasters, crime, rehabilitation, gun control, urban politics, child welfare, the American family system, and, most recently, extreme poverty and homelessness. There is a consistent ideological theme that runs through these miscellaneous topics, namely, a strong concern to improve our society by providing the best possible knowledge about its pressing problems. I am deeply concerned with issues of equality, political liberty, and personal choice. I got into evaluation research because I saw a way in which I could bring together my technical skills and my political interests in an effort to find workable and effective solutions to social problems.

Current Crisis in Evaluation

The current crisis in the evaluation field concerns seemingly radical differences in what evaluation is, its epistemological base, how evaluations should be conducted, the accepted meanings of validity and meaning, and views of the purposes of evaluation. Simplifying drastically, on the one side, there are the advocates of qualitative methods, of abandoning what they believe to be the positivism of their rivals, and, in evaluation activity, of paying special attention to stakeholder interests, especially those of the clients of programs. And, on the other side, are the partisans of quantitative methods, which are based on research models transferred from the mainstreams of academic social science disciplines, advocating randomized field experiments, emphasizing standardized data collection and reproducibility of results, and oriented more to policymakers than to other stakeholders.

In the current qual-quant polemics in evaluation, the history of the conflict is often glossed over. This conflict has a long history, ranging back at least to the period of the first growth in the social sciences in the early decades of this century. Each generation of antagonists has added nuances to the conflict, but the basic terms of disagreement remain fairly constant over the decades. To dub current qualitative fashions as "fourth generation" is to make a discovery out of a refurbishment.

In my home base discipline, sociology, the struggle between the quants and quals is alive and well today, but it has been alive and well since sociology first turned away from being an armchair discipline and started to undertake empirical investigations. When I was a graduate student in the late 1940s, the conflict was between the case study or life history approach versus sample surveys; it exists currently as an often rancorous debate between symbolic interactionists and so-called positivists.

In sociology, I believe that the quals consistently have outnumbered the quants. Nevertheless, over the decades, the quants have tended to win more of the positions of power, prestige, and influence within the profession. Although I have made no counts, I estimate that the quants have won the majority of the elected positions in the American Sociological Association and have dominated the editorial boards of the mainstream journals and the professoriate at the major research universities. In the most prestigeful of the professional journals, research articles based on qualitative research are outnumbered by those based on quantitative studies, by a ratio on the order of ten to one. In addition, the majority of the grants and contracts go to the quants.

The quals tend to predominate among the teachers, especially of under-graduate courses, among the undergraduate textbook writers and the writers of the few best sellers that sociologists produce. Sociology does not have much of a clinical practice, but what little there is strongly supports the quals.

As an organized profession, evaluation is just a few decades old, so the conflict between the quants and quals in this field is not exactly an ancient conflict, although it can be called persistent, being a continuing theme in our professional meetings and in the literature. In the AEA, the victories of one side or the other have not been clear-cut. Certainly, the quants get the big evalua-tion contracts and serve as editors of the major journals in the field, but the elected officials do not seem to come predominantly from one side or the other. In contrast, the evaluation quals appear to predominate among those who do small-scale, local evaluations. In general, quals are more closely identified with the management of programs and with clients. In some substantive fields, for example, educational evaluation, the quals appear to have the upper hand.

All that said, what this persistent division signals to me as a sociologist is that in order to understand these differences, we have to examine the struc-tural arrangements that they reflect and that sustain them. By structural arrangements I mean the ways in which evaluation research is socially orga-nized, including the market for evaluation research, the segmentation of that market, the organizational arrangements for the conduct of evaluations, and the roles played out within those arrangements. Of course, not everything is determined by or reflects structural arrangements: There are critical intellec-tual problems that are also involved and hence deserve some discussion as well, although I do not examine these problems in this chapter.

Historical Roots of the Crisis in the 1960s

The 1960s are usually credited as the time when evaluation research came into its own. Starting in the 1960s and continuing through the 1970s, there was a great boom in new social programs fueled by an enthusiastic optimism that our society, through proper social policy and the funding of effective govern-ment programs, could increase general well-being, provide for the unfortunate, and lessen inequality.

The social programs started in the 1930s were judged more on their ide-ological worth. In contrast, those launched in the 1960s were judged on effec-tiveness and improved until maximally efficient. Social science knowledge was given the role of guiding the design of programs, and social research that of estimating their effectiveness. I have often puzzled why the idea of using social science knowledge and social research methods became acceptable and even popular in Congress and in the executive branch in the 1960s. I like to think that it was because the social sciences flourished in the postwar undergradu-ate curriculum and infiltrated the professional schools, especially law schools, but I suspect that the full explanation is a lot more complicated.

Whatever the reasons, the 1960s boom meant that demand for evaluation research was high enough to foster the development of an evaluation industry and corresponding evaluation profession to meet that demand. Social scientists in some quantity began to undertake policy-related social research on a fairly large scale.

We learned a number of important lessons by being plunged into the policy arena: First, we learned that evaluation tasks were formidable: Paraphrasing Millicent Fenwick's aphorism that "old age is not for sissies," we can say with some heat that evaluating is not for sissies either. There were many booby traps and pitfalls to be encountered on the way, some technical, others organizational, and still others political. Elegant evaluations were hard to design, equally hard (perhaps even harder) to implement, and the resulting evaluations often were not gratefully received by all.

Second, we learned that evaluation was not going to dominate the policy process. Although some of us may have entertained hopes that in the "experimenting society" the experimenter was going to be king, that delusion, however grand, did not last for long. It often seemed that programs had robust lives of their own, appearing, continuing, and disappearing following some unknown processes that did not appear responsive to evaluations and their outcomes. For example, despite the fact that evaluations found at best marginal effectiveness for job training programs, these programs are still around, designed in much the same way for decades. The same statements can be made about programs that attempt to rehabilitate felons, and so on.

Third, we discovered that many initially very promising programs were at best marginally effective. We learned that doing good was hard work, all the way from program design through implementation, to achieving effects. It was a humbling experience to learn that basic social science had little, if anything, to offer in the design of programs, mainly because public policy and accompanying social programs had so little impact on behavior that social scientists usually ignored policy variables in conducting basic research.

In the early 1960s, the ruling stance of evaluators was that others would design programs and we would evaluate them as given. Initially, we left the design of programs to policymakers and administrators. However, we quickly discovered that there was very significant work to be done on program design. We also learned that treating programs as if they were black boxes was wasteful; it did little good to learn how effective a program was because that fact did not say much about why it was effective (or not) and told little about whether the program could be implemented successfully at other sites. We learned that in many cases programs were ineffective seemingly because they had not been implemented or had been implemented incompletely or incorrectly. Accordingly, the scope of evaluation activities was enlarged to include formative activities in support of the design and process research on the implementation of programs.

Finally, despite the first three discoveries, evaluation became more and more fashionable: Evaluators may have despaired about evaluation, but policymakers became increasingly committed to it. Evaluation requirements routinely became written into most social legislation. Accordingly, evaluation research was sponsored and funded on federal, state, and local levels, sometimes under the duress of federal mandates. Perhaps the ultimate signal of success came in the 1980s when the General Accounting Office (GAO), long a bastion of green eyeshades and pencil sharpeners, opened a new division with the mission to develop an evaluation capacity.

I find it difficult to understand the steady support for evaluation in light of its mixture of successes and failures. But that is an insider's viewpoint, more influenced by the realization of failures than by the glory of its successes. For surely there were great successes: James Coleman's early work on equality of opportunity, the several income maintenance field experiments, and the highly regarded work of Eleanor Chelimsky's shop in GAO, to mention just a few. But maybe the proper response is just to accept the fact that evaluation has become an integral part of the welfare state, enjoy that status, and work as hard as we can to deserve it.

The end result was the development of a new field, evaluation research, complete with its own professional associations, professional journals, and training programs. Before the 1960s, there were social scientists who did evaluations, but there were few, if any, who considered themselves primarily as evaluators. Now there is an evaluation profession and an evaluation industry, whereas before there were, at most, ad hoc evaluation teams.

What these four developments started is still affecting us today. First, the difficulties encountered in carrying out evaluations led to close examination of the theory and practice of evaluation and eventually to an expansion of the scope of evaluation to encompass more than impact assessment. The debate between the quants and the quals is an expression of that search for better approaches to evaluation. And so is the current exploration of selection bias modeling as a viable alternative to randomized field experiments. To the research question, "Does the program have any outcomes attributable to it?" we have added the questions, "How can we design programs that have a good chance to be effective?" and "How can we get ordinary agencies to run the programs properly?"

Second, the difficult logistics of carrying out mandated large-scale evaluations led to a segmentation of the industry into, on the one hand, an oligopoly consisting of a handful of very large firms that consistently win the big contracts for the large-scale evaluation of federal programs and, on the other, a much larger pool of small firms and solo practitioners handling the smaller evaluation tasks. Given the heavy capitalization needed to enter the ranks of the oligopoly, it is not likely that the major leagues will grow greatly by adding additional large firms. In contrast, all one needs to be a small-scale evaluator is a minimal track record to establish credentials, a letterhead, a fax machine, and a personal computer with a good word-processing program on it.

Third, the failure of programs to prove more than slightly effective also had an impact. For some, this disappointment led them to question the rationales for the programs that were tested. When I first met Charles Murray, he was the principal investigator on an evaluation being carried out by the American Institutes for Research, the outcome of which was to find an ineffective program. I venture that that experience affected the development of his conservative criticism of social programs. Others raised questions about evaluation methodology: Maybe the programs were all right but we did not know how to show that was the case. Still others questioned whether YOGA—Your Ordinary Government Agency—could run effective programs.

Some of the major federal agencies began to lose nerve. If effective programs could not be easily developed on the national level and imposed on state and local agencies, then why not get local and state agencies to do the development task? Surely, out there in the hinterland there must be some schools, police departments, social agencies, public welfare units, and so on who are doing it right? All we need is to foster diversity and effort, and those on the firing line who know the problem intimately will come up with effective solutions. Surely the grass is greener and smarter at the roots?

I find this development very disturbing. The grass roots do not constitute the habitat for the intellectually strongest part of the social welfare establishment and are certainly not a stronghold of social science. Good programs do need to earn the allegiance and enthusiasm of local agencies and frontline personnel, but local agencies are not the best sources of effective new programs. In addition, local agencies often lack the broad perspective to understand the structural roots of our social problems.

Fourth, the realization that evaluators were not going to be philosopher kings also had implications. Undoubtedly, some with royal aspirations drifted away. The realization gave rise to a cottage industry devoted to finding out what influences evaluations have had on the political process. I am sure we are all relieved to discover that we are not totally irrelevant but a part of a process of knowledge creep.

Many evaluators, however, shifted the search for rewards from the political process to the program process. If policymakers and high administrators will not let us sit at the high table, maybe some other table will have us. If we helped a program to function better, then evaluation is worthwhile. And how could we tell whether we helped? If the program evaluated, its clients, and other major stakeholders are happy with the evaluation, then is that not enough? Of course, this shift of reference groups also meant deemphasizing impact assessment and becoming more involved in providing informed consultation on the running of programs. I return to this point later.

Fifth, the greatest impact came from the growth in the total amount of evaluation activity. The big glamorous national contracts were out of reach of nearly all outside the big firms, but there was plenty of small-scale stuff. State and local evaluation opportunities were plentiful: School systems, police departments, public welfare agencies, and private agencies all either wanted to have evaluations done or were mandated to do so by their funding sources. In many cases, these were opportunities to do fine work, but in many others, if not a majority, the evaluation efforts were hard to carry off well under the condition of being badly underfunded, often an afterthought. And yet many of the evaluations had to be undertaken in some form in order to fulfill the legislative mandate.

These developments have led to strong differentiation in the tasks faced by evaluators in actual practice, leading in turn to differentiation among evaluators. In short, the different kinds of evaluation tasks faced by evaluators have led to different styles of evaluation and to correspondingly different evaluation ideologies.

Strains in the Structure of Evaluative Tasks

The evaluation tasks that face us vary widely on a number of dimensions. Here, I point to a few dimensions that I consider crucial, each conditioning strongly the kind of evaluation approach that can be taken.

Perhaps the most important dimension of all is scale: The task facing someone who wants to evaluate a nationwide program is markedly different from the task of evaluating a small local program. For example, evaluation of the welfare-to-work programs that were started in many states after the welfare reform act of a few years ago clearly presents a different order of problem from that of evaluating the efforts of a program to reduce dropouts in a Springfield, Massachusetts, high school. Even with the assistance of every graduate student at my command (as if I did have them at my command!), there is no way I could take on the task of evaluating more than one state's welfare-to-work program using any form of evaluation methodology. At that, evaluating the program in one state would seriously strain my resources. A national program requires more of an organizational capacity than I could possibly muster.

But the situation facing a qualitatively inclined researcher is very different. If a qual wanted to bid on a contract to evaluate welfare-to-work programs in a number of states, there is no way he or she could use qualitative approaches in dealing with the task as defined as a multistate evaluation, even if the request for proposal (RFP) would allow it. The high level of expertise required for fieldwork at its best, or even just at an adequate level, means that the evaluator would have to assemble a fairly large crew of quite talented fieldworkers in each of the states. And that would likely mean more than just one person in each state. I believe that the fairly well paid crew size would be quite large, have to be committed to the fieldwork task for an extended period of time, and hence be very expensive.

As a consequence, the conduct of large-scale, multisite evaluations is largely in the hands of the big research firms such as Mathematica, Manpower Development Research Corporation, Abt Associates, Research Triangle Institute, the Urban Institute, and the National Opinion Research Center. It is noteworthy that the dominant discipline in most of the big firms is economics, a decidedly minority presence in the membership of AEA.

In contrast, I can take on the school dropout program evaluation in Springfield, Massachusetts, much more easily and have more degrees of freedom in designing the evaluation. I could recruit one or two graduate students, perhaps involve a colleague or two, and carry out the task. Furthermore, the evaluation could take on a variety of forms. It could be based primarily on fieldwork, with my assistants and myself talking to students, teachers, parents, employers, and so on before, during, and after the program and coming out with a report that presents the program from the several viewpoints involved. I could also carry out a randomized experiment in which students at high risk of dropping out are assigned randomly to experimental and control conditions.

Alternatively, I could undertake both qualitative fieldwork and a randomized experiment and hope that I could somehow integrate the two approaches in my report to the Springfield school system. There is a lot that I am glossing over in this account so far, especially the difficulty in carrying out an uncorrupted experiment in that environment. I would have to deal with the school board, the high school administration, the teachers who run the program, the students, and so on through the litany of stakeholders involved. If I took the qualitative road, I would also have the same stakeholders to deal with but in a more passive mode. That is, I would not have to convince them of the propriety of randomization. And, in the end, in which way would I do best? I suspect that I could help the Springfield school system more if I provided it with the best qualitative-based report than if I presented the best possible randomized experiment and a brilliant analysis of findings. I also believe that I could help them even more if I presented them with both the best experimental and qualitative findings and I integrated the two sets of findings.

Now, all of this is hypothetical and unlikely to occur, especially the melding of the two approaches. There are several reasons why melding is not likely to happen, but the most important reason is the fiscal constraints. It would indeed be highly unusual to have enough money allocated to fund both a randomized experiment and fieldwork. The odds are that fieldwork would be the approach eventually taken for several reasons: First, fieldwork ordinarily appears to be cheaper. Second, a randomized experiment takes much more time to complete. Finally, there are few who could successfully carry off both an experiment and a fieldwork excursion, and there are even fewer who could successfully meld the two sets of findings.

There have been several large-scale evaluations that have had fieldwork components built in, but those were add-ons, more a concession to the image of qualitative work than a truly serious integration or a primary effort. As far as I know, there have been no large-scale evaluations in which qualitative methods were at the center of the evaluation efforts.

A second dimension of differentiation among evaluation tasks lies in the source of and control over funding for evaluations. At one extreme, the impetus and funding for an evaluation come from the lofty reaches of policy-making and upper levels of agency administration, far from the trenches. For example, Congress may mandate that the Department of Housing and Urban Development (HUD) undertake an experimental evaluation of housing vouchers, or the Department of Health and Human Services may decide to evaluate adolescent pregnancy prevention programs. The agency then draws up a RFP, advertises its existence in the Congressional Register, and then waits for bids to come in. In this process, there typically is little or no role to play for the state agencies, let alone local agencies or clients.

At the other extreme, the impetus comes from sources much closer to the front lines, from program managers or from other lower levels of administration. For example, a local social agency may receive funds from HUD to run an innovative, transitional housing program for homeless families. In order to get the grant, the local agency had to promise that the program would be evaluated. Shortly after receiving the grant, the agency director asks around to find out whom he or she might approach to undertake an evaluation. Having found a willing evaluator with an acceptable evaluation plan, the agency enters into a contract for the evaluation. Alternatively, the agency might want to add someone to their staff or reassign a current staff person to the evaluation role. In either case, the connection between evaluator and the organization being evaluated is very close.

Because funding sources write the RFPs, their influences on the definition of the evaluation are clear from the start. High-level funding sources do not often specify all the stakeholders who should be consulted about the evaluation and its conduct. After all, on a national level, how does one define in any specific sense who are the clients (targets) whose views should be taken into account? The general rule may be stated that the more distant the stakeholders from the funder, the less their views count.

At the other extreme, when funders are located closer to the trenches, there is likely to be more attention paid to a variety of stakeholders because funders regard such stakeholders as important and are in contact with them frequently. An agency head has to pay some attention to case workers, a principal to teachers, and so on. It is no surprise that evaluations funded by the lowest levels of our health-welfare-education industrial complex are more sensitive to stakeholder issues.

A third critical dimension is whether the evaluation is ex ante or ex post, that is, whether it is a pilot test of a program that is being considered for widespread adoption or whether the evaluation is of an ongoing implemented program. Ex ante evaluations, ceteris paribus, are easier to carry out: The program designer surely has a strong stake in how the evaluation will come out, but other potential stakeholders may not be so committed. There are other conditions that foster more formal evaluation designs. For one thing, the task of identifying comparison groups is easier when, to begin with, no potential client is receiving the program treatments. No one is worse off by being in a control group.

In contrast, evaluations of ongoing, already implemented programs are more difficult to do. For fully implemented programs that saturate their clientele groups, any kind of comparison group design is simply out of the question. Even when saturation has not occurred, appropriate comparison groups that are free from obvious selection biases are difficult to identify. Evaluations of established programs typically present political problems as well. There are always stakes held in the continuation of a program. Evaluating an existing organizational structure is like rattling the cage of an eight-hundred-pound irritable gorilla; it needs to be done very carefully!

Finally, there are considerable differences among evaluation tasks in resource constraints. To paraphrase Milton Friedman, there is no such thing as a free evaluation. To which one might add, there is also no such thing as an instantaneous evaluation. Good evaluations, qualitative or quantitative, take time and cost money. Moreover, there is a positive correlation between the amounts of resources available and the quality of the resulting evaluation that is both statistically and substantively significant, holding the scale of the evaluation constant.

These four axes of differentiation among evaluation tasks are not orthogonal: There is some correlation among them. Large-scale evaluation tasks tend to originate higher up in the decision hierarchy, are usually better funded, and are given more time for completion. In contrast, small-scale evaluations tend to be controlled by levels closer to the trenches, to be poorly supported, and to have short time lines to completion.

How the Task Conditions the Approach

The main consequence of differentiation among evaluation tasks is corresponding differentiation among evaluators. I have already noted that there is no way that a cost-effective qualitative evaluation can be mounted on a scale large enough to meet the needs of national programs. Consequently, such evaluations have become the exclusive province of large-scale research firms and are likely to be heavily quantitatively oriented. The smaller-scale evaluations have then become the territory over which is waged the battle between the quals and the quants, a struggle in which the quals are winning out.

In part, the victories of the quals is a matter of the quants leaving the field. There is no way in which I could respond in good conscience to the RFPs I receive for the evaluation of small programs in western Massachusetts. The issue of conscience arises out of my judgment that the time and funds allocated for the task typically fall far short of what I believe would be necessary to do a reasonable job, as I define what is reasonable. It is also often a matter of my judging that the programs are not worth evaluating because they are so small that net outcomes, even if large, could never be detected statistically.

In part, the victories of the quals over the quants is a matter of the quals delivering a product that is useful to the program operators. In many cases, I would not call the product an evaluation, but then an evaluation, in my terms, may not be what the program operators really need. Qualitative evaluations at this level, at their best, are often connoisseurial judgments, based on extensive practical and theoretical knowledge, further illuminated by a rich and intimate knowledge of the program in question and its ecology. In many cases, the evaluator brings to the task a comparative perspective because he or she has knowledge of other comparable programs. As well, the evaluator may have command of critical substantive and theoretical knowledge that can serve to improve a program or solve one or more of its problems.

It is important to keep in mind that connoisseurial evaluations are a familiar mode in a variety of clinical circumstances other than the evaluation of programs. This is the mode used in peer reviews for tenure, by editors of professional journals in assessing submitted manuscripts, by universities when they review academic departments and programs, and by physicians when they audit the quality of medical care. These are all circumstances in which, we hope, wise and judicious women and men bring to bear knowledge of best current practice to make an assessment of whether a particular person or organization is up to snuff, often making recommendations on how to improve performance.

All of the above can be very valuable to a program and its stakeholders. However, in my view, this is not evaluation but more like management consultation. It goes under the guise of evaluation possibly because so many programs are required to have an evaluation component. Of course, my judgment means that I am applying a particular definition of evaluation: My definition is that evaluation is the application of social science knowledge and research methods to estimating the efficiency and effectiveness of a program. Connoisseurial evaluations may involve the application of social science knowledge, but they ordinarily do not lead to defensible estimates of efficiency and effectiveness.

Of course, there is an arbitrary quality to definitions. Anyone can define a term to mean exactly what he or she wants it to mean. But there are also constraints on the arbitrariness of this process. We cannot depart too much from customary usage in arriving at definitions, if we want to be understood by others. The fact that we are all in the AEA is one indication that most of us think that evaluation covers a wider range of activities than my definition covers. Accordingly, I am willing to give up my definition in the face of such consensus (if it exists), but I believe that it is worthwhile to recognize that the term covers at least two quite disparate activities.

Crisis in Evaluation Reinterpreted

The current crisis in the evaluation discipline arises from the fact that beneath the struggle on the ideological level there is a largely unrecognized division of the field into two major parts:

Connoisseurial evaluation consists of those whose evaluation activities center around providing connoisseurial judgments, usually to small-scale programs, delivering them on a timely and inexpensive basis.

Net-outcome evaluation consists of those whose evaluation activities aim toward establishing estimates of the effectiveness and efficiency of programs, usually as applied to fairly large programs.

Of course, these two rubrics do not cover all evaluation activities. One major category of evaluation activity that is not fully covered comprises those extremely valuable descriptive studies of program implementation, so-called process evaluations. For present purposes, I put this form of evaluation aside.

Note that I do not contend that the one mode is better than the other. Both are valuable. Both are appropriate in the right circumstances. Both can be done very well or very poorly. A mechanically performed net-outcome evaluation unilluminated by rich knowledge about the program being evaluated, about program clients, and about the ecological surrounds of the program is a bad evaluation. Likewise, a connoisseurial assessment of a program undertaken by someone who commands little substantive knowledge about the topic, who is uneasy conducting fieldwork, and who simply guesses what might be most pleasing to his or her sponsors is also a bad evaluation. Each approach is subject to abuse and corruption in the hands of fools and villains, and each approach is bound to fail when applied in inappropriate circumstances.

I do not know whether connoisseurial evaluations or net-outcome evaluations are more easily corrupted. On the one hand, connoisseurial evaluation is more an art form, less easily taught, and therefore not subject to fully articulated standards of good performance. On the other hand, because quantitative methods can be more easily taught, we can judge more easily whether individuals know their stuff as number crunchers. But technical virtuosity also means that quantitative methods can be applied in a mechanical fashion that produces pyrotechnic numbers that have little or nothing to do with the reality of the program being evaluated.

If, as I contend, there are firm niches in the evaluation ecology for connoisseurial and net-outcome evaluations, then what is the struggle between the quants and the quals all about? Why does each camp not occupy its own niche, browsing peacefully on its appropriate turf? As I see it, although there are niches that are distinct, there is also a wide territory to which both modes can make claim. Accordingly, the struggle centers on those evaluation tasks that can be done one way or the other, middle-size programs that are not full coverage where the possibility exists to construct comparison groups and in which there are clearly desired outcomes.

If the market for evaluations of middle-size and small programs were governed primarily by price considerations, the qualitative evaluators would quickly dominate the market. I do not completely understand why qualitative evaluations should be less expensive, because it seems to me that a good qualitative researcher should be as expensive as a good quantitative evaluator. The main cost difference lies in the longer time needed for the latter and the employment of many more data collectors. A good impact assessment may take years to conduct and cost many magnitudes more than a good connoisseurial evaluation. In addition, the latter's report will typically be available years sooner. The fact that the less expensive qualitative evaluation does not dominate the middle-size market means that those who procure evaluations know that the products are different. If people want an impact assessment, they purchase from the quants. If they want good advice about their program and how to improve it, they buy from the quals.

I am tempted to offer the seemingly attractive compromise that in cases in which either method is appropriate, we do both, assigning an outcome evaluator and a connoisseur to the evaluation of middle-size programs. But that would be a fatuous suggestion given that resources available typically could not cover both. Another seemingly attractive compromise is that we meld the two approaches, every outcome evaluator becoming a connoisseur and every connoisseur becoming an expert in randomized and quasi experiments, but that is also fatuous at least for the current generation of evaluators.

My modest proposal is that we simply let the struggle go on, with the important modification of providing the sponsors of evaluation with the knowledge to make informed choices. Both types of evaluators should inform potential clients in full about the kinds of services they will get by choosing one or the other and the kinds of services they will not get. Accordingly, connoisseurial evaluators can tell a potential sponsor that the aim of a connoisseurial evaluation is to make a judgment about whether the program is proceeding according to best practices in the field, identifying the strengths and weaknesses in the program as revealed in consultations with stakeholders as well as indicating that defensible estimates of net effectiveness will not result from that effort. Correspondingly, the net-outcome evaluator might state that the end result would be a defensible estimate of net effectiveness but that there may be little information about how the program might be improved by fine-tuning.

I am convinced that the struggle between the quants and the quals masks a struggle over market share. Both sides may be guilty of false advertising. Qualitative evaluation of the connoisseurial sort is not the prime product for every circumstance and for every program. Correspondingly, there are many circumstances in which it would be fatuous to attempt an impact assessment. Statements that claim otherwise, whether stemming from the quants or the quals, are simply imperiously silly.

I would be marginally more comfortable within the AEA if it were composed primarily of quantitative, net-outcome evaluators. But I am comfortable enough as it stands. I could be made very uncomfortable by imperialist claims to the whole of evaluation by the quants or by the quals. I would like to see us recognize that we are up to different things, that each approach is valuable in its own right, and that each has its proper place in the evaluation scheme of things. Failing that, I would favor the establishment of separate professional associations. But my hope is that the parting of the ways never comes to AEA!

References

Rossi, P. H., and Freeman, H. E. Evaluation: A Systematic Approach. (5th ed.) Newbury Park, Calif.: Sage, 1993.

Shadish, W. R., Jr., Cook, T. D., and Leviton, L. C. Foundations of Program Evaluation: Theories of Practice. Newbury Park, Calif.: Sage, 1991.

PETER H. ROSSI is Stuart A. Rice Professor Emeritus in sociology and director-emeritus of the Social and Demographic Research Institute at the University of Massachusetts, Amherst. He is past president of the American Sociological Association and the recipient of several honors for his work in evaluation.

Neither methodological correctness nor paradigm purity offers an
appropriate framework for evaluation practice.

Qualitative Plus/Versus Quantitative: The Last Word

Mary Lee Smith

When Rothman and Olson (1992, p. 48) reported the results of the New American Schools Development Corporation competition, a noted policy researcher denounced the absence of money to fund comparative studies to evaluate the effects of the new designs. The practice of not funding control groups studies, he was quoted as saying, "was reprehensible. . . . All they'll have is stories—and great stories and very interesting stories—but stories."

This news report provides an appropriate backdrop for considering the tension in the evaluation community between qualitative and quantitative approaches. Experiments or stories: which offer the preferred or even the best possible framework for evaluation practice? Or does the dialogue show that we are in the midst of paradigm wars or generations in conflict (Lincoln, 1991; Sechrest, 1992)?

History of Methodological Correctness

Many of my generation cut our teeth on Campbell and Stanley (1966), where we learned that the comparative experiment was the only way to settle competing claims in educational and social policy. Alternatives such as case studies represented misspent efforts.

At that time, there were few alternatives to this perspective on evaluation. We honed our design skills on Cook and Campbell (1979) and mastered complex factorial designs and several ways of rejecting the null hypothesis. For whatever reason—a desire for certainty, a need to demonstrate our mastery of complex skills of numeracy, the elegance of the experimental logic, our unexamined assumptions, or cognitive dissonance—we accepted the premise that the results of the true experiment (or as close as we could come, quasi-experimentwise) were the last word in evaluation knowledge. We believed in the definitive experiment. Random assignment was the key to objective, unbiased methods, which in turn were the keys to truthful results. Internal validity was central. An evaluation study was well done if it reduced the uncertainty about whether the outcomes of a program could be attributed to the program.

But history caught us. Experiments built up, but their results failed to add up. Individual experiments conflicted with one another, failed to reject the null hypothesis, or were ignored systematically by policymakers.

So some of us turned to research synthesis. If we had to give up hope for the decisive experiment, we still could believe in the definitive meta-analysis. Although the methods were certainly less exacting than those of the primary experiment, they were predicated on the desire for objective, systematic methods as the key to valid results. After five hundred comparative studies on the effects of psychotherapy (Smith, Glass, and Miller, 1980), for example, we expected to pronounce the last word on the subject. Although the data proved robust enough to support the overall average benefit of psychotherapy, the variation in effects was substantial, even among studies with similar surface characteristics. This pattern of results suggested that local contingencies and complexities had obscured the main effect. Substantive evaluation concerns such as the relationship between therapist experience and psychotherapeutic effects could not be teased apart, even from a collection of studies of this size. On issues of most concern to clients and consumers, even meta-analysis failed to provide the last word.

For my generation, then, the assumption about the relationship between quantitative approaches and truth was shaken by this record of applications. The belief in methodological correctness and the definitive finding has been further undermined by critiques of quantitative studies on their own terms. Rosenthal (1978) and Rosenthal and Rosnow (1969) recorded instances of confirmatory bias, reactive arrangements, and experimenter effects in experiments. Cronbach (1975) and Meehl (1986) pointed out the fallacies and weak inferences forthcoming from Fisherian hypothesis-testing procedures. Meehl (1978) highlighted the ancillary assumptions often hidden in quantitative approaches and responsible for what he called the "slow progress in the soft sciences." One does not have to subscribe to the "other" paradigm to critique quantitative methodology.

Methodological critiques and analyses of the politics of evaluation (Weiss, 1977) suggest that although quantitative methods are meant to control subjectivity, they can address only certain varieties of subjectivity. Decisions about what to examine, which questions to explore, which indicators to choose, which participants and stakeholder to tap, how to respond to unanticipated problems in the field, which contrary data to report, and what to do with marginally significant statistical results are judgment calls. As such, they are value-laden and hence subjective, with codes of practice but no system of procedural rules sufficiently complex to cover all possibilities.

Although experimental designs are intended to control bias, they are capable of controlling only one type of bias, such as the assignment of the least disturbed patients to the preferred therapeutic treatment group. They speak not at all to the kinds of bias represented by the funding agency's decision to evaluate treatment A rather than treatment B, the evaluator's bias in reporting those findings that placed treatment A in the best light and in burying the rest, or the agency's decision to censor the findings or, if politically favorable, to proclaim them as holy writ. To the doubters, I offer the reaction of the Bush administration's educational policymakers to the Sandia Laboratory studies that showed public schools were not doing so badly (censorship) and to the Chubb and Moe (1990) regression coefficient on the superiority of private schools (ecstatic overinterpretation). (For analyses of these studies and reactions to them, see Berliner, 1992; Glass and Matthews, 1991.) Overall, the degree of bias that one can control through random assignment or blinded assessment is a minute speck in the cosmos of bias.

As the edifice of quantitative methods showed cracks, methodologists disagreed on the standards of truth that can emerge from evaluation studies. Cronbach (1975) viewed the world of evaluation practice as one of complex contingencies and mediating factors operating in different contexts that are not adequately captured in main effects and producing interactions that do not generalize in patterned ways. But the study of these complexities requires that the evaluator be present and develop an understanding of local conditions and of what makes the program work where it does work and impedes its effectiveness in other settings. The view of the world explicit in Cook and Campbell (1979) is simpler: The treatment is a single, molar entity that can be introduced and manipulated. One determines the statistical effects of the program but does not look closely at what makes it work. Cronbach seeks to examine and elucidate the workings themselves, even if one must forgo some design and statistical niceties in the process. For Cronbach, external validity, whether the effects of the program hold up under variations of the program as implemented, is more important than local molar descriptive validity (Cook, 1991). Thus, the results of the evaluation study cannot be restricted to a simple test of a null hypothesis but instead require personal involvement, observation, and interpretation—in short, some less than objective and detached methods and less than definitive results. No last word. The split between Campbell and Cronbach on the priorities to be assigned to different conceptions of validity demonstrates that alternative views of truth are possible, and these compete for acceptance in an arena of professional practice. The door is thus open to other standards for evaluation results: structural corroboration (Eisner, 1991), ecological validity (Bronfenbrenner, 1977), catalytic validity (Lather, 1991), and consequential or systemic validity (Messick, 1989).

Nor is reduction of uncertainty about the causal claims of the program the sole goal for which evaluators may legitimately strive. In evaluation research, the questions of greatest relevance are most often "What happened here?" "How did it happen?" "What preceded it?" "What followed it?" "What did it mean to those present?" These questions are logically prior to questions of causality.

Take as a hypothetical example the desired (Rothman and Olson, 1992) comparative study of New American Schools Development Corporation schools. To make either formative or summative judgments about the worth of one of these schools, decisions to fund or deny funding, to maintain, modify, or disseminate, terminate, or adopt it in other sites, one almost always needs to know what went on in the name of that program. Having found out what it is and how it works, where it fits in organizational, political, and social contexts, one might at some point want to know its overall effect and range of effects. As is often the case in public and educational policy, however, the political climate necessary to implement programs of this type disappears before proper comparative studies of their effects can be conducted (Weiss, 1982). Would the political agenda for the New American School have outlasted the experimental trial meant to test its effects? Or is a story of its existence the most an evaluation can hope for in such cases? Calling for large, complex experiments over the range of models is nothing more than asking to repeat the follow through evaluation experience (House, Glass, McLean, and Walker, 1978).

Perhaps my generation is losing its memory. A historical reading of evaluation practice suggests that even correctly done, "scientific" studies failed to settle policy disputes, guide program development, or deliver truth, particularly on the questions that begin with "what" and "how." Many of us who were disillusioned with experiments and other hypothesis-testing, causation-seeking studies found greater satisfaction with qualitative approaches in which the evaluation researcher could be sensitive to local context, participant interpretations, historical and cultural structures interacting holistically, and social actions and processes. We were drawn to the kinds of evidence that can only be gained through firsthand, long-term observations and interactions of researcher with participants. We borrowed methods from anthropology, sociology, and even journalism and the arts. We were willing to cede some internal validity to gain authenticity, unit generalization for analytical and naturalistic generalization, objectivity for Verstehen. For some of us, this was a fair trade in spite of accusations that we are numerical idiots or mere storytellers. Justification for such an evolution only requires a view of society as complex, a view that one person's experience of program X and interpretation of indicator Y might differ from those of another's, and a recognition that evaluation methods are fallible.

History of Paradigm Purity

Disappointment with traditional hypothesis-testing approaches and a growing affinity for fieldwork were not sufficient to rationalize a turn toward qualitative evaluation. Academics require philosophies to justify practice. Some found that justification in an alternative worldview—constructivism, interpretivism, hermeneutics. These philosophical positions hold that the world is a social construction inseparable from the minds that make it up, that all knowledge is particularistic and relative, and that all accounts are equivalent (see, for example, Guba and Lincoln, 1989). The bogey was "positivism," a word I set off in quotations because what counts as positivism is still the subject of debate (see, for example, Eisner, 1983; Phillips, 1983). Positivism is something like pornography, not readily defined in the abstract but apparent when encountered in the particular.

Qualitative evaluation then seemed to be divided into theoretical and practical camps, some doing it and others talking about it. Most journal space on topics of qualitative evaluation has been spent on clarifying the philosophical underpinnings of the constructivist paradigm; which approaches, questions, and methods fit; and, more to the point, which should be purged as associated with positivism.

The push for paradigm purity extended particularly to studies using mixed methods. Energies were spent in the philosophical debates about incommensurability and incompatibility (Howe, 1988; Smith and Heshusius, 1986). Practice was neglected or consigned, like practice in other professions, to the realm of personal knowledge, gossip, or, at most, conference proceedings.

The fascination with paradigms has had several consequences. First, the intentions and assumptions of evaluators are confused with the methods they use, a confounding of ideas and tools. An experiment might be based on traditional notions of the relationship between objective methods and truthful outcomes and intended to narrow the definition of problem space and close out the argument about the worth of the program. That particular evaluator might gloss over contradictions and value differences in the name of focus and methodological correctness. A different evaluator might pick an experiment as a way to clarify causal dynamics, to remove an especially problematic alternative hypothesis, and to open debate about the worth of the program. The results of the experiment would be used in the context of other information and a variety of perspectives. There is one tool in both examples (each done to exact specifications) but two different sets of intentions and beliefs. One must examine cases—instances of practice—and question the values and assumptions that the evaluator held and the consequences of holding them. It is less useful to reproach a class of methods in general. Nor does it make sense, even for constructivists, to reject wholesale the quantitative studies on such substantive issues as tracking or retention, merely because their authors were positivists. Instead, one must consider those studies as provisional and subject to debate about their truthfulness and possible application to particular instances.

Second, in assuming no connection between correct methods and true accounts, extreme constructivists have seemingly abandoned the search for the warrant for qualitative accounts. Although objectivity, reliability, and unbiasedness have been amply demonstrated as problematic, rationality, rigor, and fairness can still be sought. No all-purpose, general set of standards for qualitative practice can be specified in advance. However, methodologists can reflect on the characteristics of their own and others' studies to discern the qualities that make them credible and useful. Qualitative and mixed-method evaluators have not done enough of this kind of work. We need to be examining instances more fully and coming to an understanding of what we do that promotes equitable interactions with participants and stakeholders, trustworthy and contextually credible accounts, and authentic representation.

As a start, let me state what I look for: a sense that the evaluator was present over a long enough time period and close enough to the action and to participants' meanings; informed by some system of theoretical ideas about the social and educational substance of the program; adept at the ethical, political, and personal relationships that qualitative methods make inevitable; successful in sampling widely with multiple indicators and methods; adept at forms of representation; oriented toward challenging standard hypotheses and assumptions; self-critical and amenable to the scrutiny of the field, peers, participants, and stakeholders; and able to penetrate to an understanding of the matters at hand. I offer these criteria while acknowledging that the use of any or all of them does not somehow corner the truth.

Third, the logical consequence of the mandate that qualitative evaluators avoid quantitative methods (those associated with positivism) is that evaluators restrict themselves to critical contemplation of the program, journalistic storytelling, and dialogue with stakeholders. Although these are desirable features of evaluation, they tend to take evaluators out of the conversation with policymakers and program managers. Many evaluation clients need representative surveys or assessments of comparative program benefits. For the qualitative evaluator to reject the questions, the methods, or the contract itself is to miss a great opportunity: to play an educative role not only about the substance of the program but also about the methods and their limitations (for example, how surveys gloss over multiple meanings and experiments decontextualize actions and distort effects). It is the chance to teach clients and stakeholders (many of whom are positivists or naive realists) how to deconstruct empirical studies on their own terms and engage in discussions about empirical findings and value implications. Avoidance, in the name of paradigm purity, of contracts that demand quantitative methods leaves clients and projects to less thoughtful evaluators and perpetuates the notion that numbers have magical properties.

The stand of the constructivists—that since realities are multiple, truth relative, and accounts equally true or false, the best we as evaluators can do is to produce journalistic narratives—begs the question of rigor and rationality, effectively takes evaluators out of the conversation, and obviates the necessity to do good. It is an escape from responsibility and action.

The stand of the positivists that the only valid accounts are those graced with objective, methodologically correct procedures (all other methods besides controlled, quantitative, deduction being preliminary, biased, or fallacious) is at best false advertising and self-interested. It denies the complexities of social life and the recognition of context sensitivity that even its adherents claim for their everyday lives. Its principles lead to distortion and oversimplification and sacrifice relevance for a narrow definition of causation, objectivity, and rigor. The framing of our work as objective and unbiased is more an advertisement, a statement of commerce rather than a statement about the nature of reality. Without the appeal to an objective, value-neutral methodology, the voice of the evaluator has not much more authority than the voice of the prophet, the teacher, the preacher, or the therapist.

What is left is a move toward multiple methods and approaches in an evaluation study or the commission of a series of independent studies varying in methods. The rationale for such a recommendation and the warrant for the findings have been made elsewhere (Cronbach and others, 1980; Greene, Caracelli, and Graham, 1989; Mathison, 1988). Perhaps not every evaluator can or is willing to take on multiple approaches within a study, but he or she can promote, sponsor, draw on, integrate the findings of, negotiate over, and critique the methods and inferences of multiple approaches (each critiqued on its own terms). This is the only path to rapprochement and true synthesis in the field. It is the recognition, above all, that in social science inquiry, there is no last word.

References

Berliner, D. C. "Education Reform in an Era of Disinformation." Paper presented at the annual meeting of the American Association of Colleges of Teacher Education, San Antonio, Tex., Feb. 1992.

Bronfenbrenner, U. "Toward an Experimental Ecology of Human Development." American Psychologist, 1977, 32 (7), 513–531.

Campbell, D. T., and Stanley, J. C. Experimental and Quasi-Experimental Designs for Research. Skokie, Ill.: Rand McNally, 1966.

Chubb, J. E., and Moe, T. M. Politics, Markets, and America's Schools. Washington, D.C.: Brookings Institution, 1990.

Cook, T. D. "Clarifying the Warrant for Generalized Causal Inferences in Quasi-Experimentation." In M. W. McLaughlin and D. C. Phillips (eds.), Evaluation and Education: At the Quarter Century. Chicago: National Society for the Study of Education, 1991.

Cook, T. D., and Campbell, D. T. Quasi-Experimentation: Design and Analysis Issues for Field Settings. Skokie, Ill.: Rand McNally, 1979.

Cronbach, L. J. "Beyond the Two Disciplines of Scientific Psychology." American Psychologist, 1975, 30 (2), 116–127.

Cronbach, L. J., and others. Toward Reform of Program Evaluation: Aims, Methods, and Institutional Arrangements. San Francisco: Jossey-Bass, 1980.

Eisner, E. W. "Anastasia Might Still Be Alive, but the Monarchy Is Dead." Educational Researcher, 1983, 12 (5), 23–24.

Eisner, E. W. The Enlightened Eye: Qualitative Inquiry and the Enhancement of Educational Practice. New York: Macmillan, 1991.

Glass, G. V., and Matthews, D. A. "Are Data Enough? (A Review of Politics, Markets, and America's Schools)." Educational Researcher, 1991, 20 (3), 24–26.

Greene, J. C., Caracelli, V. J., and Graham, W. F. "Toward a Conceptual Framework for Mixed-Method Evaluation Designs." Educational Evaluation and Policy Analysis, 1989, 11 (3), 255–274.

Guba, E. G., and Lincoln, Y. S. Fourth-Generation Evaluation. Newbury Park, Calif.: Sage, 1989.

House, E. R., Glass, G. V., McLean, L. D., and Walker, D. F. "No Simple Answer: Critique of the Follow Through Evaluation." Harvard Educational Review, 1978, 48 (2), 128–160.

Howe, K. R. "Against the Quantitative-Qualitative Incompatibility Thesis, or Dogmas Die Hard." Educational Researcher, 1988, 17 (8), 10–16.

Lather, P. Getting Smart: Feminist Research and Pedagogy Within the Postmodern. New York: Routledge & Kegan Paul, 1991.

Lincoln, Y. S. "The Arts and Sciences of Program Evaluation." Evaluation Practice, 1991, 12 (1), 1–7.

Mathison, S. "Why Triangulate?" Educational Researcher, 1988, 17 (2), 13–17.

Meehl, P. E. "Theoretical Risks and Tabular Asterisks: Sir Karl, Sir Ronald, and the Slow Progress of Soft Psychology." Journal of Consulting and Clinical Psychology, 1978, 46 (4), 806–834.

Meehl, P. E. "What Social Scientists Don't Understand." In D. W. Fiske and R. A. Shweder (eds.), Metatheory in Social Science: Pluralisms and Subjectivities. Chicago: University of Chicago Press, 1986.

Messick, S. "Validity." In R. L. Linn (ed.), Educational Measurement. (3rd ed.) New York: American Council on Education and Macmillan, 1989.

Phillips, D. C. "After the Wake: Postpositivistic Educational Thought." Educational Researcher, 1983, 12 (5), 4–12.

Rosenthal, R. "How Often Are Our Numbers Wrong?" American Psychologist, 1978, 33 (11), 1005–1008.

Rosenthal, R., and Rosnow, R. L. (eds.). Artifact in Behavioral Research. San Diego: Academic Press, 1969.

Rothman, R., and Olson, L. "Researchers See Little New Knowledge from 'New Schools.'" Education Week, Aug. 5, 1992, pp. 48–52.

Sechrest, L. "Roots: Back to Our First Generations." Evaluation Practice, 1992, 13 (1), 1–7.

Smith, J. K., and Heshusius, L. "Closing Down the Conversation: The End of the Quantitative-Qualitative Debate Among Educational Inquirers." Educational Researcher, 1986, 15 (1), 4–12.

Smith, M. L., Glass, G. V., and Miller, T. I. Benefits of Psychotherapy. Baltimore: Johns Hopkins University Press, 1980.

Weiss, C. H. "Introduction." In C. H. Weiss (ed.), Using Social Research in Public Policy Making. Lexington, Mass.: Lexington, 1977.

Weiss, C. H. "Policy Research in the Context of Diffuse Decision Making." Journal of Higher Education, 1982, 53 (6), 619–639.

MARY LEE SMITH is professor of educational policy studies at Arizona State University, Tempe.

Debating the merits of qualitative versus quantitative approaches is a useless endeavor unless we carefully specify terms; once this is done, it is obvious that most of the approaches are complementary.

The Quantitative-Qualitative Debate: Possibilities for Integration

Terry E. Hedrick

The exchanges between quantitative and qualitative program evaluation advocates have become increasingly pointed and accusatory during the past three years. Recent presidents of the American Evaluation Association (AEA) have held very strong opposing views about the merits of these approaches and have communicated these views to the AEA membership in very direct terms (Lincoln, 1991; Sechrest, 1992). Debaters have defined the issue in exclusionary terms, either relegating quantitative researchers to the status of dinosaurs or lamenting the numerical illiteracy of qualitative researchers. It is, therefore, no secret that the speakers at the 1992 AEA annual meeting were chosen in the hope of both clarifying the terms of the debate and, perhaps, of even identifying a common basis for understanding. Thus, when the planners of the 1992 conference issued an invitation to me to be a plenary discussant, I eagerly accepted. Only slight trepidation arose when I received the following reactions from two colleagues: The first said, "What! Is that old issue still being discussed? Hasn't it all been said before?" And the second said, "What! You shouldn't have agreed to be a discussant on this topic; talking on this topic is a no-win-situation. Whatever you do, don't say what you really believe." Neither colleague was optimistic about the outcome of the 1992 AEA discussions.

Enjoining this debate is no minor challenge. The quantitative-qualitative frameworks are not uniformly defined and applied across the field, and both are continuing to evolve (Datta, 1992). Yet I believe that having this discussion is extremely important for three reasons. First, as an organization, we must be able to identify and define our basic underlying values. As evaluators, we have difficult new issues to work on—especially in light of the challenges of new domestic program agendas—issues that require us to work together if we are to succeed. We cannot afford to be divided as an organization. Second, some sort of resolution of the debate is important to our ability to maintain external credibility with our customers: all consumers of evaluative information. If so much effort is devoted to challenging the merits of different schools of thought within the profession, how credible can the profession be to others? Third, resolution of the debate is important for our future, to our ability to train and prepare students to enter the evaluation profession. As the pendulum swings back and forth between quantitative and qualitative, we risk losing the opportunity to prepare and train individual graduate students in the richness of both traditions.

I was reassured at the 1992 AEA meeting when Ernest House set the ground rules for this discussion in his opening remarks. He called for productive debate on the quantitative-qualitative topic but acknowledged that it is acceptable for such debate to be emotional. As a predominantly quantitative evaluator, I survived being labeled a dinosaur without experiencing undue emotional upset; however, recently I came across an education journal article that made reference to the persisting "vestigial" remnants of quantitative evaluation (Howe and Eisenhart, 1990). That reference raised my blood pressure. Being labeled a dinosaur is not a problem. Dinosaurs are liked by both children and adults, dinosaurs have made impressive comebacks in recent novels and movies, and, frankly, dinosaurs are seen as powerful large animals that have had quite a lot of influence. But a "vestigial" remnant is not very exciting or attractive at all. According to Webster's New World Dictionary (Neufeldt, 1990), a vestigial remnant is a "trace" of something that has "passed away," for example, the remaining signs of a tail on homo sapiens. Therefore, I confess to a certain degree of personal emotional involvement in the discussion of this topic.

In the spirit of the qualitative evaluators, I begin by stating my own bias. As someone who has conducted small- and large-scale program evaluations both in government and in the private sector, and as someone who currently has responsibility for the training and education resources provided to about three thousand evaluators at the U.S. General Accounting Office (GAO), I lean heavily toward the quantitative perspective. Yet, I value many aspects of the qualitative paradigm and methods and advocate their combination with quantitative approaches and, at times, their use alone. My perspective undoubtedly is shaped by my environment. The congressional requestors for GAO's evaluation work generally want to know about program compliance, efficiency, or effectiveness; they want facts about program impacts as well as relative trade-offs. And the language of these evaluations is a numerical, and therefore quantitative, language.

What Do We Mean by Quantitative and Qualitative?

Before debating the merits of quantitative versus qualitative evaluation, we must clarify our terms and distinguish what we mean by quantitative and qualitative, for the terms often are used very loosely to refer to a wide range of philosophies and methods. Talking about the relative merits of quantitative versus qualitative in the abstract is absolutely meaningless. In this regard, it is helpful to distinguish between the more global notions of paradigm and design versus the more specific notion of method (see Table 5.1 for examples).

Table 5.1. Examples of Paradigms, Design Approaches, and Methods

Term	Quantitative	Qualitative
Paradigm	Positivist (scientific method) approach	Constructivist (fourth-generation) approach
Design	Experimental Quasi-experimental Representative samples Case study	Hermeneutic dialectic Pattern matching Case study
Method	In-person interviews (structured) Questionnaires Observational recording Administrative records	In-person interviews (unstructured) Focus groups Thick description Observational recording

The term paradigm in Table 5.1 refers to the philosophy or school of thought underlying the research approach; in its most extreme contrast, it is the positivist paradigm versus the constructivist paradigm. These paradigms represent very different views of the nature of knowledge and the role of the evaluator. Positivist evaluation approaches rooted in the scientific method seek to increase the likelihood of objective, unbiased answers by relying on the research procedures that have proved successful in the physical sciences. The attendant role of the evaluator is one of information provider to decision makers. Thus, the evaluator becomes an advocate only for responsible use of the results and prizes neutrality and objectivity. On the other hand, the constructivist-based researcher starts with the premise that objectivity and value-free science are impossible and believes that the scientific method is an outmoded approach to evaluation. The constructivist seeks to play an active role in program decision making by building consensus among the parties as to what needs to be done. The goal is one of bringing about change and empowering all stakeholders.

The most relevant question for our debate is whether these paradigms can coexist within the same study. In these extreme forms, the answer is no. There is little room for compromise between quantitative and qualitative research frameworks. Neither approach recognizes the legitimacy of the other, and attempts to combine them are illogical. It is on this level that the debate takes its most exclusionary form. (Note that extreme examples of the paradigms are described here to highlight the degree of contrast possible between quantitative and qualitative approaches; there are other paradigms, such as "realism," that fall somewhere between the two extremes. Realism recognizes the time-bounded nature of evaluation information and the existence of different perspectives on programs, but it also strives for validity and reliability of measurement and replicability of study execution.)

The term design in Table 5.1 refers to how an approach handles issues of causal attribution and representativeness. Quantitative study designs generally adopt approaches such as experiments and quasi experiments that rely on the scientific method for determining causality, using design or statistical approaches to rule out alternative possible explanations. Or such studies may strive to estimate the pervasiveness of an opinion or factor (either within the study context or more broadly); in these cases, sampling procedures and projection methods become especially important. The constructivist paradigm, however, advocates study design approaches that value the reality of all stakeholders equally; such studies base causal conclusions on the congruence of perceptions expressed during consensus-building processes (the hermeneutic dialectic process) and place heavy emphasis on reaching agreement on what changes should be made in a program. This type of qualitative researcher may not place much importance at all on determining the pervasiveness or frequency of particular opinions or factors or outcomes in large populations.

Qualitative researchers are far from homogeneous, however; some qualitative researchers use the scientific method of hypothesis testing with qualitative data. A good example of this is the pattern-matching approach advocated by Miles and Huberman (1984). Also, case studies can be portrayed as either quantitative or qualitative. When an evaluator conducts separate experimental impact studies in multiple locations, these are often referred to as quantitative case studies. And some qualitative case study researchers using nonnumerical data adopt the underlying logic of the scientific method (see Yin, 1989) and engage in hypothesis testing, while others rely instead on providing rich descriptions from which the reader may draw his or her own conclusions.

Can these quantitative and qualitative design approaches coexist in the same study? The answer depends on the specific approaches, but, yes, it is definitely possible and probably desirable to integrate them.

Finally, the term method in Table 5.1 refers to how data collection occurs and what form the data take; the key factor is whether the data exist in a quantitative or qualitative form. Generally, quantitative methods are focused on obtaining specific items of information, and great stress is placed on systematic approaches across people or places; qualitative methods are more likely to involve techniques that broaden the information base—adding more perspectives, raising additional issues, constantly accumulating more details, with less attention to inconsistencies in data collection procedures. Again, this is not always a straightforward distinction, for many kinds of qualitative data may be transformed to quantitative through coding and frequency counts of qualitative phenomena. An example of this transformation is the use of content analysis, a procedure for systematically coding the presence or absence of certain words or themes in textual or spoken material. Such material is thus transformed into frequencies, enabling us to perform quantitative analysis.

Can quantitative and qualitative data collection methods and forms be used in the same study? Absolutely yes, we do it all the time and the integration greatly enriches our studies.

The point of all this is that the terms qualitative and quantitative are not sufficiently explanatory in and of themselves to serve as the basis for debate. Each is applied to a broad array of paradigms, designs, and methods that have commonalities and differences that may bear little or no relationship to these labels. At the broadest level, that of paradigms, the approaches are more likely to be mutually exclusive; as we move to consideration of the levels of design approaches and methods, it becomes easier to envision the approaches used together in a complementary manner.

Three Doors: Choices for the Evaluator

In considering possibilities for integration, I find it useful to think of the evaluator as having three potential sources to turn to when considering how to conduct an evaluation study. These sources can be portrayed as doors to workshops, each filled with tools.

As we face these doors, we face choices in the conceptualization, design, and execution of our evaluation studies. Unlike contestants on "Let's Make a Deal," we already have some idea of what is behind each door. We can decide, for example, that certain doors are more useful to open for certain kinds of studies than for others. And, finally, again unlike "Let's Make a Deal" contestants, we need not make forced choices; we can open more than one door at once. And, in fact, our studies may be greatly improved if we open doors 1 and 2 simultaneously.

Door 1: Quantitative. Behind door 1, under a global heading of quantitative, can be found a wide array of tools—from experimental and quasi-experimental designs executed on a national scale or in selected locations (quantitative case studies) to sample surveys of opinion and observational recordings (frequency counts) of behavior. All share the same foundation; all approaches assume that it is possible, indeed desirable, to attempt to reliably "measure" some aspect of the real world. And the making of causal attributions is achieved through hypothesis testing and the systematic exploration (through research design or statistical analysis or logic) of alternative possible explanations for what occurred.

Evaluators using these approaches recognize the risk of bias creeping into study designs, and in fact they may admit that it is not possible to do value-free research. However, they take careful steps to minimize bias to the greatest extent possible.

Door 2: Qualitative. Behind door 2, under a global heading of qualitative, can also be found a wide array of tools—from extensive processes to determine the perspectives of stakeholders to qualitative case studies with thick descriptions of contexts, events, and views, to rich responses to open-ended interviews. Many of these qualitative approaches rest on the same foundation as those behind door 1. For example, efforts are made to ensure that field observers are sufficiently trained to make reproducible, reliable observations. Causal inferences are based on qualitative data, but such inferences are held to the same standards as for quantitative data: time precedence, covariation, and nonspuriousness. Pattern-matching approaches are used in data analysis. Open-ended interviews are done with representative samples of program participants, resulting in rich summaries of views that are representative of persons receiving services. Because the tools behind doors 1 and 2 have the same foundations—construct validity, internal validity, and external generalizability—they are easily combined within a single study.

Door 3: Behind door 3 is another workshop, a workshop built on a different foundation from the other two. Guba and Lincoln (1989) call it fourth-generation evaluation; I see it as having some commonalities with organizational development work. It sees value-free science as impossible, reaches conclusions on a consensus basis, and believes that data are time-bounded. "The peculiar web or pattern of circumstances that characterizes a given situation may never occur in just that way again, so that explanations and management actions are in a real sense unique and cannot be understood as implying either predictability or control. . . . Explanations are at best 'here and now' accounts that represent a 'photographic slice of life' of a dynamic process that, in the next instant, might present a very different aspect" (Guba and Lincoln, 1989, p. 98).

Given my setting, I do not open this door to use its design and method approaches, for its utility is extremely limited for my setting and the credibility of its findings is too vulnerable. It does, however, stimulate thinking about a variety of potential biases concerning how we plan studies: what questions we choose to address and whose perspectives may go unaddressed. It may also be useful in more formative evaluation settings where what is needed is more programmatic technical assistance, consultation, and facilitation of communication among funders, program staff, and clients.

Possibilities for Integration

Many of the members of AEA are already successfully integrating quantitative and qualitative approaches. As the brief "show of hands" survey I conducted during the 1992 AEA plenary session indicated, the vast majority of conference attendees considered themselves about equally balanced between quantitative and qualitative approaches. Also, during the meeting, we saw many examples of evaluation research that integrated these approaches. They ran the range from a quantitative analyst who included an implementation variable in a regression equation estimating program outcomes to an evaluator of an after-school program for youth who appointed an anthropologist as part of the research team. We are still not completely comfortable with the integration, but we are doing it anyway. In this regard, let me describe how quantitative and qualitative approaches are integrated at GAO.

Developing an Understanding of the Issues. When requested by a congressional committee to conduct an evaluation study, one of the first things we train staff to do is to develop a thorough understanding of the issues of concern and to identify the specific questions that must be answered. This process includes talking with relevant parties: the congressional members or staff, agency officials and management, visits to programs, discussions with groups that favor or disfavor the program, program clients, and so on. Such activities generally involve gathering qualitative data about the program's history, culture, operations, and context in ways that help the team plan and design the research. It is during this process that we identify the original goals for the program and sometimes identify concerns about unintended effects of programs that bear further investigation, for example, fears that the Internal Revenue Service policy of keeping the tax refunds of persons who have defaulted on their student loans might lead to greater tax noncompliance (and therefore revenue loss) in subsequent years.

Understanding Multiple Perspectives When Developing Measures. Measurement development is a critical feature of sound program evaluation work: What should be measured and how? During the design phase of many studies, GAO teams need to become familiar with the various perspectives of stakeholders in a program (the program funders, the program management, the program staff, the program clients, and so on) and develop interview, survey, or observational approaches to gather meaningful data. Immersing oneself in the setting over an extended period is one way to acquire this type of familiarity; but this approach is not practical given our tight time frames for doing work. Instead, we often conduct focus groups as a first step in questionnaire or interview development. This practice of bringing together people to discuss a set of questions about a program, policy, law, or regulation has the advantage of allowing the evaluation team to check if they have identified the most relevant issues and to hear the language and terms people bring to the discussions. Thus, if the team listens carefully, it can use the experience to design better measures—measures that capture the full range of perspectives on a program.

Understanding the Factors That Affect Program Implementation. Programs do not exist in isolation; they are housed within larger delivery structures and cultures. Our staff need to be able to anticipate what the major stumbling blocks may be for a new program, to understand the intricacies of federal, state, and local relations regarding a program, and to understand the importance of agencies' cultures and historical missions as potential mediating variables that can affect program effectiveness. Additionally, the success of a modification of a program may depend on whether the reward structures that exist for program staff and clients are consistent with that change, as well as the informal norms governing behavior. An example of this type of situation exists in the area of inventory practices for the Department of Defense. It is widely known that the federal government has extensive and costly inventories greatly in excess of service needs stored all over the United States. One factor in this is a culture that rewards "never running out" of anything as opposed to "achieving maximum efficiency in ordering and storing supplies." Changing this type of practice requires changing the culture of agencies, not just changing regulations. This kind of information is most likely to be picked up during open-ended and relatively unstructured interviews—in other words, through a qualitative research methodology.

Interpretation of Data and Reporting. Finally, a lot of criticism is lobbed toward quantitative researchers about presenting analytical results in unfriendly, technical language. Personally, I know of few researchers who speak this way any more. Instead, we try to speak straightforwardly, such as "Earnings for women were only two-thirds that of men." We speculate as to the reasons for our results, we tell what we know, and we offer hypotheses for why. These kinds of judgments require knowing the program's context, understanding the full range of forces at work, and understanding all parties' perspectives. Anecdotes may even be used to illustrate what the more representative analytical results are telling us. These kinds of statements require qualitative knowledge about the program's functioning.

In sum, the integration of qualitative and quantitative approaches goes on all the time at GAO; doubtless there are many more opportunities than those mentioned here. Even in GAO's quantitatively oriented environment, it is thus possible to integrate these approaches effectively. As House (1992) said, "We are restricted only by our ingenuity and our resources." I expect and look forward to seeing more demonstrations of integrated research at future AEA meetings.

References

Datta, L. "Paradigm Wars: Can We Give Peace a Chance?" Paper presented at the annual meeting of the American Evaluation Association, Seattle, Wash., Nov. 1992.

Guba, E. G., and Lincoln, Y. S. Fourth-Generation Evaluation. Newbury Park, Calif.: Sage, 1989.

House, E. R. "Integrating the Quantitative and Qualitative." Paper presented at the annual meeting of the American Evaluation Association, Seattle, Wash., Nov. 1992.

Howe, K. R., and Eisenhart, M. "Standards for Qualitative (and Quantitative) Research: A Prolegomenon." Educational Researcher, 1990, 19 (4), 2–9.

Lincoln, Y. S. "The Arts and Sciences of Program Evaluation." Evaluation Practice, 1991, 12 (1), 1–7.

Miles, M. B., and Huberman, M. Qualitative Data Analysis: A Sourcebook of New Methods. Newbury Park, Calif.: Sage, 1984.

Neufeldt, V. (ed.). Webster's New World Dictionary. New York: Warner Books, 1990.

Sechrest, L. "Roots: Back to Our First Generations." Evaluation Practice, 1992, 13 (1), 1–7.

Yin, R. K. Case Study Research: Design and Methods. (Rev. ed.) Newbury Park, Calif.: Sage, 1989.

TERRY E. HEDRICK is director of the Training Institute at the U.S. General Accounting Office.

Both qualitative and quantitative paradigms have contributed much to evaluations. Both, however, are works-in-progress with many issues still unresolved and assumptions incompletely tested. Further, both are more similar in practice than might be expected from the sometimes strident disputes—all grounds for peaceful coexistence and for going beyond to a new perspective.

Paradigm Wars: A Basis for Peaceful Coexistence and Beyond

Lois-ellin Datta

Here are three images. The first is of two sumo wrestlers. The second image is of a candidate for sainthood. As the candidate advances from the status of a fine person who does much good, to beatification, to canonization, to sainthood, the evidence required gets more and more demanding. To mix the images, if one of those two sumo wrestlers is a saint, we should all get behind and push; if not, maybe they both should get more training. The third image is of three evaluators standing by an ocean whose life forms they seek to understand. The first evaluator holds a state-of-the-art rod with a big quantitative hook. The second evaluator holds a finely meshed qualitative net. And the third evaluator is a scuba diver.

The Wrestlers

Recently, presidents of the American Evaluation Association, speaking for themselves and for members who shared concerns with them, sent signals that seemed to indicate if not a state of war, then at least a condition of stridency (Guba and Lincoln, 1989; Lincoln, 1991; Sechrest, 1992; Fetterman, 1992). One signal from the qualitative perspective said, "Your paradigm is history." A riposte from the quantitative perspective was, "Don't you call me a dinosaur, you innumerates." And another signal could be read as saying, "But we honor dinosaurs if they talk nicely."

From one historical perspective, it is surprising to see two paradigms, like sumo wrestlers, trying to push each other out of the ring. From another historical perspective, the current paradigm wars were predictable.

A History of Coexistence

There are at least five reasons to be surprised at the stridency: (1) both approaches have been used for years, (2) many evaluators have endorsed appropriate use of both paradigms, (3) even federal agencies thought of as quantitative seem comfortable with qualitative approaches, and vice versa, (4) both have had policy impacts, and (5) both have taught the field of evaluation so much.

Both Paradigms Used for Years. For about as long as I can remember, quantitative, qualitative, and mixed-model evaluations have coexisted. In the early days of the U.S. Office of Economic Opportunity, for example, there were quasi-experimental designs (for instance, both the Westinghouse-Ohio study and the Head Start Longitudinal Study conducted by the Educational Testing Service used quasi-experimental designs). There were mixed-model designs, such as the classic Head Start Community Impact Study. There were qualitative studies, such as Greenberg's The Devil Wears Slippery Shoes, a report on the Mississippi Community Action Program, which also is a classic, and the Dittman-McDaniels case studies of individual children in Head Start planned variation.

Some evaluations worked out well, others worked out badly. The ones that worked out badly often got blasted. The next round of evaluations usually tried to build on the good experiences, avoid the pitfalls, and work toward new approaches.

Many Evaluators Have Urged Using Both Paradigms. Early on, evaluators called for bringing together quantitative and qualitative approaches. Table 6.1 lists, chronologically, only a few of the relevant studies. As early as 1973, Sieber was discussing the integration of fieldwork and survey methods. By 1981, Louis was able to present new approaches, tried out in field evaluations, to integrating quantitative and qualitative methods.

Leading theorists from both qualitative and quantitative persuasions looked to using both in the same evaluation, often as different methods for answering different questions. For example, Campbell (1974) discussed qualitative knowing as part of action research. Cook and Reichardt (1979) edited a widely read book on qualitative and quantitative methods. Fetterman has included in many of his books chapters discussing multimethod research (see, for example, Fetterman and Pitman, 1986).

Agencies Have Supported Both Paradigms. At the federal level, sometimes one paradigm has predominated, sometimes another. Often, there are notable differences from agency to agency at the same point in time. For example, in the 1970s, when the U.S. Department of Education was emphasizing randomized and quasi-experimental designs, the National Science Foundation education offices emphasized case studies.

Generally, mixed models increased in popularity. This was partly due to their virtues, as people became more aware of the importance of linking process and product. Partly, mixed models were one way of getting around an

Table 6.1. Earlier Calls for Using Both Paradigms

Year	Authors and Abbreviated Titles
1959	D. T. Campbell and D. W. Fisk "Multitrait-Multimethod Matrix"
1972	R. Rist "From Disdain to Detente"
1973	S. Sieber "Integration of Fieldwork and Survey Methods"
1974	D. T. Campbell "Qualitative Knowing in Action Research"
1979	T. Jick "Mixing Qualitative and Quantitative Methods"
1979	M. J. Trend "Reconciliation of Qualitative and Quantitative Analyses"
1979	T. D. Cook and C. S. Reichardt "Qualitative and Quantitative Methods"
1981	J. Farley "Combining Quantitative and Qualitative Methods"
1981	K. S. Louis "Integrating Qualitative and Quantitative Methods"
1982	D. Madey "Benefits of Integrating Methods"
1982	A. G. Smith and K. S. Louis "Multimethod Research"
1983	J. K. Smith "Attempt to Clarify the Issue"
1986	M. L. Smith "The Whole Is Greater"
1986	J. K. Smith and L. Heshusius "Closing Down the Conversation"
1987	G. O. Martin "Uses of Qualitative and Quantitative Methods"
1987	M. M. Mark and R. L. Shotland "Multiple Methods"
1989	R. K. Yin "Case Study Methods"
1992	S. Levitan "Evaluation of Federal Social Programs"

Office of Management and Budget (OMB) requirement that all data collection efforts involving more than nine subjects be gruesomely reviewed by OMB (Datta, 1982).

Even at the U.S. General Accounting Office (GAO), case studies of many varieties have become an accepted option for program results audits. These studies have included an examination of the effects of legal alien farmworkers on wages and working conditions of U.S. farmworkers, which combined a survey of the basis for setting wages, an economic analysis of these approaches, and four in-depth ethnographic case studies of working conditions in industries such as tobacco and sugar beets (General Accounting Office, 1988).

As a rough estimate, about a third of the GAO's nonfinancial audits (that is, audits of program implementation, compliance, and results) involve some type of case study. The price of acceptability within GAO for case studies is the same as it is for any method: an emphasis on study quality, including documentation of the basis for all statements and findings in a report that can be checked independently through a quality-assurance process called "indexing/referencing." Subjectivity, in the sense of using as data the impressions of the evaluatee and evaluator, does not in itself create problems for the agency; bias does. "Case studies, like any other method GAO uses, have to meet two criteria of impartiality: accuracy and lack of bias in the sense that the evaluator's personal, preconceived opinions about the situation do not distort reporting and that the evaluator is scrupulously even-handed in examining all sides of a situation" (Datta, 1990, p. 65).

Both Paradigms Have Influenced Policy. Further, both quantitative and qualitative studies have influenced public policy decisions, as well as local program development. With regard to quantitative approaches, Boruch (1987) extensively studied examples of randomized designs that have proved feasible to carry out (Greenberg and Shroder, 1991) and have affected decisions across astonishingly diverse areas. Even Weiss (1993) has taken a mellower tone, concluding that evaluation is contributing to incremental changes in policies. As one example of the impact of such an analysis drawing on an ethnographic study, Fetterman (1988) gave a fascinating history of his work on programs for gifted and talented students, which led to clear policy recommendations and much attention to his findings. National policy, such as initiation of a center for research on gifted and talented students and the decision to define gifted and talented more broadly than academic prowess, can be traced to Fetterman's work. The influences of evaluations from either paradigm are, of course, not always direct or homogeneous, but both have proved policy-useful (Fetterman and Pittman, 1986; Fetterman, n.d.).

So Much Has Been Taught by Both Paradigms. Both paradigms have contributed notably to the way in which we think about evaluation. Table 6.2 summarizes some lessons taught by each, lessons in part learned through the hard work of evaluators trying to improve their art, craft, and science. For example, today, evaluation standards call for stakeholder involvement, and

Table 6.2. Lessons Taught by Qualitative and Quantitative Paradigms

Lesson	Qualitative	Quantitative
Questions	Involve stakeholders Multiple perspectives	Pay attention to policy questions
Design	Look at the whole event in context	Examine nested multiple foci
Data	Study meaning and history	Collect multiple measures
Design	Emphasize implementation and process	Emphasize design power and sensitivity
Attribution	Try to rule in most information; try to explain variability, do not dismiss it as error	Seek energetically alternative interpretations and rival hypotheses and try to rule them out; estimate relative influences
Analysis	Triangulate and look for patterns	Look for interactions
Reporting	Focus on the user and utilization	Aim for methodological transparency

many evaluations begin with trying to understand what different—make that many different—stakeholders see as the issues. That is a lesson taught to us all by qualitative methodologists. As another example, evaluation standards call for methodological transparency, making public what the evaluator did in the conduct of the study: measures, instance selection, data reduction and analysis, precautions taken to achieve quality, and limitations and strengths. That is a lesson taught to us all by quantitative methodologists.

Why Our Current Debates Were Predictable

There were three elements that, as we look back, we might have seen would lead to a schism: brass knuckles, Ronald Reagan, and mixed-up models.

Brass Knuckles. Much of the debate in the field of evaluation has been conducted with energy, but without anyone getting badly hurt. Some people, however, felt real pain. For example, a National Research Council panel was charged with synthesizing the results of the twelve-foot shelf of evaluations of the Youth Employment and Development Programs Act, funded in the late 1970s by Robert Taggart and his colleagues at the U.S. Department of Labor. The panel, in an earnest effort to draw what they believed would be justified, generalizable conclusions, applied a gold standard of randomized designs and found that only a few studies met this standard. All the rest were disregarded for policy purposes. I have not read all of that twelve-foot shelf, but I funded some of those disregarded studies, which happened to be multisite ethnographic evaluations conducted by Rist and his colleagues at Youthwork. Those who tell me that these evaluations have no value for policy purposes have got rocks in their heads.

That is, if the panel had reviewed each study for excellence within standards of quality for the paradigm used and discarded low-quality quantitative and qualitative studies, while retaining high-quality quantitative and qualitative studies, arguably, the public interest in sound conclusions would have been achieved. What can feel like a brass-knuckles approach is when high-quality qualitative evaluations get tossed in the same wastebasket as low-quality quantitative studies, just because they are qualitative.

Using mixed-model designs for two community-based programs, PUSH/EXCELL and Cities in Schools, evaluators reported that the programs were best understood as a movement, that the Reverend Jesse Jackson inspired the youth to whom he spoke, but lacking any follow-up, the youth were not demonstrably better off or the schools more responsive than before. Qualitatively oriented evaluators tore these studies to pieces. Eventually, the attacks were perceived as so personally virulent that one principal investigator, who felt unable to get a fair hearing, left our field.

Ronald Reagan. In 1981, the nation turned aside from federal leadership on domestic issues in favor of getting federal hands off states and putting a priority on foreign relations. This was not some putsch, but the culmination, through the democratic process, of many earlier trends, including public frustration that many social problems seemed to be getting worse instead of better.

"Obliterated," "destroyed," and "eliminated" have been used to describe the thoroughness with which federal hands were lifted from many mental health, housing, environmental, and educational programs. Evaluation was among the first to go, along with crucial statistical series (General Accounting Office, 1987). Evaluation syntheses and meta-evaluation flourished as a way of being able to say something with practically nothing in the way of resources and with roads to new data collection blocked. Evaluators became skittish about how findings would be used. The stakes of a poor evaluation got higher, since it either contributed to the waste of what little money there was on ineffective programs or failed to show what was working. Increasingly, evaluators sought paradigmatic purity and a "what works," "promising practices" emphasis.

The tide may be flowing the other way. As a nation, we may be more concerned about domestic issues, not only our own employment or unemployment but also the deterioration of our cities, random violence, the environment, drugs, homelessness, domestic violence, the intergenerational consequences of big deficits, and how to deal effectively and fairly with these and other predicaments. And we yearn for someone to articulate a nobler vision, a principled vision, of what we are about as a profession.

Fourth-generation evaluation offers such a vision with an explicitness and eloquence not matched by other paradigms. In this context, criticizing the approach can be seen as not caring about social justice. However, those evaluators who do not believe that evaluation should be an agent of a particular political or social agenda, however attractive, can resent like blue blazes being regarded as uncaring agents of an oppressive regime.

Mixed-Up Models. A third factor is lack of a worldview, paradigm, or theory for mixed-model studies. Absent such a guide to development of practice and assessment of quality within a paradigm, mixed-model evaluations can seem like mixed-up evaluations. Such a theory has yet to be fully articulated, particularly in a noble vision of what we are about.

Have the Saints Come Marching In?

Defining a paradigm clearly, fairly, and completely enough to assess its claims to the throne is a necessary but difficult task. The analyses reported next were among several made, using different characterizations of each paradigm. The nuances, while surely important symbolically, did not seem to yield analytically notably different results.

Characterizing the Paradigms. With respect to the worldview associated with the qualitative paradigm, the guiding essence is the belief that subjective reality—the meaning of events to the individuals concerned and, by implication, the inherently unmeasurable—is what matters. In contrast, in the worldview associated with the quantitative paradigm, the guiding essence is that objective reality—the events that can be publicly shared and, by implication, what can be measured in some way—is what matters.

The qualitative paradigm is characterized by acceptance of subjective information and skepticism about objective measures; by emphasis on a rich, comprehensive, in-depth understanding of what has happened as the meaning of events to those involved; and by emphasis on an additive approach to explanations, in which understanding is considered complete when all the available information can be incorporated into a satisfying pattern, and there is no inconsistent information that has been ignored. The quantitative paradigm is characterized by acceptance of objective measures and skepticism about subjective information, except when interpreted as attitudes and beliefs; by emphasis on a description of what happened in the context of initial expectations and observed events; and by a subtractive approach to explanations, which are considered adequate when rival hypotheses can be ruled out through control or comparison observations, through statistical adjustments, or through an accounting of much of the observed variation.

Both qualitative and quantitative paradigms are far from monolithic. The qualitative paradigm includes approaches that take a moral position (Guba and Lincoln, 1989); those that seek to understand each culture in its own terms, trying to avoid evaluator biases (Miles and Huberman, 1984, 1989); those that are based on the sociological tradition of case studies (Louis, 1981; Yin, 1989); those that are based on adapting ethnographic traditions to policy-oriented evaluations (Rist, 1972); those that are closest to the research tradition (Wax,

1971); and those that adapt various qualitative models to practical evaluations (Fetterman, 1986, 1992; House, this volume; Patton, 1980, 1987; Greene, Caracelli, and Graham, 1989; Goetz and LeCompte, 1981). These differences within the qualitative tradition are structural, not cosmetic. It is thus not surprising that evaluators who till the qualitative field are not always comfortable with one another's approaches.

The quantitative paradigm is, if anything, even more diverse. It includes approaches based in economic methods (Heckman, 1991), those grounded in sociological methods such as survey research (Rossi and Freeman, 1993), those derived from experimental designs (Boruch, 1987), and those associated with statistical traditions (Hedges and Olkin, 1985). Again, the differences can be profound within the quantitative tradition. To say that those tilling this quantitative field are not always comfortable with one another's approaches is to engage in understatement. As a quick sample, debate aficionados may enjoy Levitan's (1992) review of the amazingly acrimonious, and intellectually quite elegant, exchanges among the randomized design, quasi-experimental design, and microsimulation design analysts on the income maintenance and manpower development evaluations of the past fifteen years. Thus, there can be so much divergence within each paradigm that some quantitative and some qualitative theorists are fairly close in worldview and methods, while others are worlds apart.

Is Either Paradigm the Mary Poppins of Evaluation, Practically Perfect in Every Way? This is not a comparative analysis, asking, for example, whether the qualitative approach to establishing influences is better than the quantitative approach to attribution. Rather, the analysis asks, within each paradigm, how well it measures up to its own standards when viewed against three questions. These three questions are not new; they are the questions applied to most theoretical statements in the social and physical sciences: (1) Is there an internally consistent framework of assumptions, principles, and arguments? (2) Are the assumptions testable? (3) When tested, how well does the framework hold up?

First, both paradigms have theoretical statements that are, by and large, internally consistent, sets of assumptions that have been articulated with considerable clarity and that seem to fit together, at least as seen by fellow evaluators. However, there are questions raised about the conceptual structures of both paradigms that even their avatars consider areas where further work is needed. For example, Lincoln (1981) and Guba (1981) grapple with issues of trustworthiness, authenticity, reproducibility, and transferability, and Berk and others (1985) and Boruch (1987) grapple with issues of attribution in quasi experimentation.

Second, both paradigms have changed so rapidly over the past two decades that clearly both are capable, if not of being disproved, at least of shaking up the people who care most deeply about their development. For example, the criticism of the qualitative paradigm as lacking in an approach to data analysis that would reduce chances of evaluator biases has been addressed in several remarkable developments. Halpern (1983) pioneered an auditing approach to the analysis of qualitative data that, if followed, promises to ensure the plausibility of steps between observations and interpretations of the meaning of events to the other people involved. Miles and Huberman (1984) took a big step for evaluationkind in bringing together ways of analyzing masses of qualitative data that made the methodology accessible to multisite projects. Their book is now in its fifth reprinting.

The quantitative paradigm, too, is susceptible to disproof, as shown by change in response to criticism. For example, the early evaluations using randomized assignment often lacked information on what might have accounted for disappointing or encouraging results. In response to justifiable criticism, assessment of implementation now is widely accepted as an essential part of the quantitative method.

But despite all we deservedly celebrate about the contributions, the incompleteness of both paradigms seems clear, an incompleteness that impairs our ability to know what to do to achieve high-quality studies. For instance, since the qualitative paradigm claims to offer more than ipsative knowledge, then more systematic work is needed on conceptualizing what is meant by reproducibility (perhaps the qualitative equivalent of external validity or generalizability) and how in this paradigm reproducibility is assessed (see, for example, the outstanding methodological series by Goetz and LeCompte on ethnography and evaluation, beginning with Goetz and LeCompte, 1981). As another example, the fourth-generation qualitative paradigm emphasizes equally social values and the meaningfulness of the perceptions of all stakeholders. When stakeholders have values antithetical to those of the evaluators, can the evaluators educate but not coerce their clients and fairly represent their values? (See, for example, Reed's [1991] analysis of evaluation based on specific political allegiances.) When time is short and the evaluators few, how are selections made among the many potential stakeholders available to be interviewed, observed, and understood? Further, how widely can the qualitative paradigm be applied? To defense evaluations? Environmental issues? Analyses of regulatory effects? Evaluations of the effectiveness of huge tax expenditures as well as programs supported through on-line budget authorization? Moreover, the conceptual and methodological basis for establishing causality through qualitative analyses of multiple-case field studies (Miles and Huberman, 1989) is still much under discussion.

The quantitative paradigm, too, has plenty of places for improvement. To mention only a few, more work seems needed on methods for imputing missing values in designs aimed at generalizability to specified populations; on appropriate controls or comparisons when communities rather than individuals are the focal units; on designs appropriate for situations where the definition of the problem to be addressed and the approaches to it are variable, flexible, and unpredictable; on the management of evaluation design when attrition is both high and nonrandom; and on how to avoid technically correct but policy-sterile designs and analysis. And this paradigm, too, is only beginning to be well tested in application to defense, environmental, regulatory, and tax expenditure analyses (beyond the econometric and time-series approaches).

Tables 6.3 and 6.4 present some of the considerable unfinished business of both paradigms, based on theoretical and conceptual sources. The conclusion? Both paradigms have claims to fame; neither is a saint, let alone God.

The Scuba Diver

Evaluation may, however, be ready to move beyond quantitative thesis and qualitative antithesis to a new perspective. Here it may be instructive to shift from theory to practice. For this analysis, the focus is on naturalistic evaluation as an example of the qualitative approach, and experimental design as an example of the quantitative paradigm. I asked Yvonna Lincoln and Lee Sechrest to identify good evaluations that well represented their approaches. Lincoln replied with great generosity, Sechrest did not receive my letter. The stand-in is a major evaluation of a large demonstration program supported by the National Institute of Alcoholism and Alcohol Abuse (NIAAA). This is being designed and conducted as a cooperative agreement among the demonstration program developers and local evaluators, NIAAA, and a distinguished national evaluation team.

Naturalistic Evaluation. Lincoln recommended seven evaluations, which she uses to show her own students what evaluations emerge from her approach. She selected studies that present development over time and that illustrate the diversity of applications. The evaluations range from a told-in-the-first-person report of therapy as experienced by a bulimic woman to an exploratory study of the effectiveness of a bilingual education program. Three were descriptions of experiences (Meyers, 1989a; Wolf, 1978; Denny, n.d.), two were formative evaluations (Wolf and Tymitz, 1980, 1981), and two were program evaluations (Meyers, 1989b; Henze, 1990a, 1990b).

Descriptions of Experiences. As an example, one descriptive study, written with great beauty and sensitivity, shares the experience of an elementary school and university science teacher who spent about three months observing and interviewing widely in the schools of River Acres, Texas (Denny, n.d.). The narrator's voice interweaves with the voices of many others, creating a truly remarkable surrogate experience, an extended visit to a school system with a wise, sensitive observer. No lessons drawn, and no questions asked and answered: The experience is shared for the readers to learn from it what they will.

The three descriptive studies are similar to the illustrative case studies that, over the past twenty years, have provided surrogate experience in scores of evaluations. GAO and many other agencies use such reports to help people who may never go down in a submarine, teach a classroom of multilingual children, or live in Watts but nevertheless make decisions affecting the lives of people who do.

Formative Evaluations. As an example, one of the studies (Wolf and Tymitz, 1980) evaluated the impact of the Hirschorn Museum and Sculpture Garden. Information on who visitors were, what they did, what they said, and impli-

Table 6.3. Areas Needing Further Work: Qualitative Evaluations

Area	Work Needed
Questions	Examination of the compatibility of the expectation of representing the culture and reality experienced by all stakeholders and the expectation that the evaluator is concerned with empowering those who are relatively unempowered in a situation (differentiation of subjectivity and bias)
Design	Basis on which stakeholders are selected when there are too many to interview or observe in a situation; definition and operationalization of standards of excellence in qualitative evaluations, and criteria for distinguishing between good and poor qualitative studies: For example, should the audit trail technique be an expected part of all qualitative evaluations? Should stakeholders be given an opportunity to comment on draft reports and have these comments a matter of public record, if they so choose?
Attribution	Development of methods for the analysis of attribution, influence, and causality in multisite evaluations
Analysis	Development of methods for the synthesis of the findings and data for qualitative evaluations; development of methods for the secondary analysis of raw data from qualitative evaluations
Reporting	Improvement of methodological transparency; development of ways for achieving the goal of reporting what has been learned in user-friendly ways, including achievement of rich, contextualized, well-written reports that also include summaries

cations for what the Hirschorn could do came from rich observations, visitor quotes, surveys, and numerical data. This approach may have been revolutionary in 1980. Now there is little distinguishing the study from what a well-trained evaluator would probably do: Refrain from a questionnaire handed out to a random sample passing through the door, use quantitative means to get demographic and factual knowledge, and observations and interviews to record actual behavior and to find out what different types of visitors thought.

Program Evaluations. The larger of the two exemplary evaluations was conducted for the Lower Kuskokwim School District of Alaska, an area including an unusually high concentration of communities where the Native American language (Yup'ik) is still spoken. The materials included a summary report (Henze, 1990b) and three case studies (Henze, 1990a; Regan, 1990; Vanett, 1990). The frameworks guiding the study are cited as systems theory, Vygotsky's approach to cognitive-linguistic development, and Cummin's theories on the empowerment of minority students. The naturalistic evaluation framework is not mentioned.

The three case studies report on brief (three- to five-day) site visits by two evaluators to three Alaska villages with bilingual education programs. The site

Table 6.4. Areas Needing Further Work: Quantitative Evaluations

Area	Work Needed
Questions	Examination of the limits of applicability, for example, in highly complex, unpredictable situations
Design	Examination of issues of overdesign, and of where the fixes needed to avert threats to design integrity and interpretability overwhelm program development
Analysis	Examination of when to stop analyzing, so that probabilities are not distorted by selecting "useful" results from thousands of discarded analyses; continued consideration of technical issues in evaluation syntheses, such as how to integrate results of mixed-model designs; recognition of and attention to systematic attrition
Reporting	Development of ways to avoid technically correct but sterile studies, replete with factoids and devoid of meaning

visitors observed classes, reviewed documents, met with students, and interviewed many people in each village. Here, for the first time in the set of evaluations, a sense of what the naturalistic paradigm might mean in practice comes through. I have read many site visit reports on bilingual education programs. Few are written as eloquently and with as much explicit attention, for a brief report, to context, program, and issues.

These reports were different, however, in three ways. First, more than usual, a philosophical or political stance was taken by the evaluator on the importance of empowerment, on best pedagogical practices, and on whose values should prevail when values clash: views announced by the selection of the three frameworks and realized in what was examined and how information was interpreted. That is, the evaluators brought to the studies strongly held views (criteria, normative expectations, judgmental frameworks) about what good practice would look like in schools. They were up-front, explicit, and clear about these views, which infused the studies.

Second, tensions and clashes were spotlighted, although the achievements, hard work, and good intentions of teachers were recognized sympathetically. This probably resulted from a decision by the evaluators not to answer the question in the request for proposals about the effectiveness of the bilingual education programs; instead, they "shifted the focus of the project in order to gain more insight into the issues surrounding bilingual education in the region" (Henze, 1990b, p. 9).

Third, the observers' personal reactions as the visits progressed were presented as information perhaps equal in importance to those of others more durably vested. For example, the main evidence given of communication problems between the district and local schools was the principals' lack of information about the purpose of the evaluation. While the question is, of course, relevant, there was no indication that the school district's view on what was communicated was sought, or that other evidence—confirming or disconfirming—on district and local communication was pursued. The summary report by Henze (1990b) runs about 120 pages: executive summary; introduction describing the purpose, framework, assumptions, limitations, and methods; description of the context of the study in terms of bilingual education issues and programs; individual case study summaries; thirty-four findings; twenty-two recommendations; conclusions; and references.

Henze (1990b) made clear that the study was a multisite, multimethod design, using questionnaires, observations, interviews, and documents. First, the evaluators made the site visits, developing initial hypotheses about what was happening and why; then they prepared questionnaires to gather relevant evidence, using them in twenty additional sites in the district. They also applied a time-series design to analyze student test score data across the district. And they put it all together, using the questionnaires, test data, document analyses, and site visit reports. The methodology would be familiar to any one of the several hundred evaluators that I estimate have taken part in carrying out such studies. The evaluators noted that "we have deliberately combined qualitative and quantitative methods in this study because each mode addresses different kinds of questions. . . . We view these two research traditions as mutually supportive" (Henze, 1990b, p. 12).

Cordray, Pion, and Associates. A design developed through the NIAAA cooperative agreement by the local evaluators, NIAAA officials, and a national evaluation team led by David Cordray and Georgine Pion may help assess what a state-of-the-art quantitative evaluation plan looks like (R.O.W. Sciences and Institute for Public Policy Studies, 1991).

To paraphrase their report, in May 1988, the first round of awards was made under the Community Demonstration Grants for Alcohol and Drug Abuse Treatment of Homeless Individuals. These awards differed from more traditional demonstrations in exploring the usefulness of many diverse treatment models, each in a different setting, rather than studying the applicability of a single model to many situations. In all instances, services usually available are always provided; the study looks at the costs and possible benefits of additional or somewhat different services. No one is denied treatment. A second round of sites responded to an announcement that continued these approaches but also specified a preference for experimental designs and specific measures. All the local studies from the second round involve some type of comparative design, and some have chosen to include case studies as supplements for their own award.

The national study depends on the sites for comparable data, but it is independent in terms of analyses, questions, and cross-site comparisons. The design derives "from imperatives of policy and subsequent dissemination . . . to include information on who is served, what services clients actually receive, how interventions are configured to achieve their intended results, and how specific programs fit into the largest services network within which they operate . . . a process-implementation-systems-outcome perspective" (R.O.W. Sciences and Institute for Public Policy Studies, 1991, Chap. 4, p. 1).

With regard to outcomes, over thirty outcomes questions are addressed, taken from the perspective of federal policy stakeholders (top down), service providers (bottom up), and cross-site (potential adopters?). As examples, top-down outcomes questions include "Did the interventions reduce levels of alcohol and other drug use among the target population?" and "What was learned about the effectiveness of interventions for the target population?" Bottom-up outcomes questions include, "What mechanisms mediate the outcomes of the interventions?" and "How do client characteristics interact with the nature and course of treatment?" Cross-site outcomes questions include, "With regard to the case management approaches, what are the effects of intensity, structure, case manager characteristics, and case manager salary?"

The national evaluation outcomes design aims at bracketing the best estimates of effects by comparing the analytical results of different, and extremely sophisticated, quantitative analyses to locate signal in the variance due to site-specific designs, nonrandom attrition, unexpectedly small or divergent N's, and other threats to power. Data include quarterly reports providing both client-level and project-level information on implementation, process, and systems; treatment services interviews with clients; a core battery of standardized assessments at the client level; cost data; logic model analysis; bimonthly telephone calls; and site visits over the three-year period. The qualitative information gained primarily from the telephone calls and the site visits is seen as integral to understanding implementation, process, and outcomes. The plan notes, "It is widely recognized even among advocates of quantitative synthesis that quantitative analyses can only go so far on their own. As the evaluation progresses, qualitative data will play a major role in guiding analysis and interpretation of the quantitative data" (R.O.W. Sciences and Institute for Public Policy Studies, 1991, Chap. 6, p. 15).

Most readers would be able to tell the difference between this design and a qualitative analysis. And most would be able to tell the difference between this design—incredibly rich in building on two decades of lessons learned about quantitative methods and the policy "imperatives" demanding multi-method studies—and the quantitative designs of the 1960s.

How the design works out in practice remains to be seen. A reader gets overwhelmed with a sort of cathedral of an evaluation structure built around a situation as extraordinarily difficult as establishing services for individuals who are concurrently homeless, alcoholic, and drug users. The effort required to develop these programs and simultaneously hold in place fairly heavyweight requirements for design and data collection could contribute to provider burnout, unless funding is truly adequate. The willingness of clients to participate not just one time, but for repeated measurements, has notable potential for systemic attrition. Further, the clients' street smarts may lead to self-selection in their preferred treatment. Other issues are whether the statistical requirements for the cross-site analytical models can feasibly be met, even with the on-paper, convincing plans for methodological triangulation. The intense contact with the sites means that the evaluators can make plenty of midcourse corrections—the imperative, in terms of R.O.W. Sciences and Institute for Public Policy Studies (1991), of using both qualitative and quantitative methods.

Peaceful Coexistence and Beyond

In this chapter, I have considered some of the lessons learned from our experiences with quantitative and qualitative paradigms. My first conclusion is that both are still too much in development to either claim or be accorded exclusive status. To move from a somewhat evangelical religion to an evaluation paradigm, the studies actually conducted under the banner of Fourth-Generation Evaluation and other qualitative approaches need to be made public with a transparent methodology. They ought to be reviewed as thoroughly as those conducted under the aegis of contemporary quantitative methods. And the latter, still much in evolution, should be tested further in practice. There is a continuing need to articulate guidelines for evaluation quality within both paradigms, keeping pace with methodological refinements and experience. This may be a basis for peaceful coexistence, probably for quite a while, as the various approaches continue to recognize and work on the methodological as well as conceptual challenges they now confront, including continuing attention to excellence in practice within the paradigms.

My second conclusion is that the differences are less sharp in practice than in theoretical statements. The best examples of both paradigms seem actually to be mixed models, even though introduced with ruffles and flourishes. Perhaps this is not surprising. First, most evaluations are conducted under many constraints. These include relatively short time frames, relatively little money, often intractable measurement challenges, scanty baseline information, wildly varying "agendas" for the studies, delays in obtaining promised funds and necessary consensus or clearances, and the need to minimize demands on others, to mention only a few. In most circumstances, evaluators have to do the best they can and need more, not fewer, approaches on which they can draw.

Second, people who do a lot of evaluations find out that the world is a complex place, where even an apparently simple question has subtle overtones. And we find out, too, that in some ways the world is a simpler place than the buzzing of unique experiences: Decisions do get made, and the evaluation results, if presented clearly, can influence these decisions. Neither the quantitative hook set for the big fish nor the qualitative net scaled for the little fish adequately captures life in most seas. We need a paradigm to help us become scuba divers.

Already, in practice, we merge, combine, mix, and adapt, using the implicit standards in theory to help establish explicit standards for practice. And we create, in actual evaluations, something that is more than a peaceful coexistence, and something that is more than one selection from column A and one from column B. Yet, the practice of mixing models solves some problems and creates others. To give just one example, drawn from the superb work of Greene, Caracelli, and Graham (1989), what is good practice in using information gathered from both quasi-experimental designs and case studies in the same evaluation? Is it equally acceptable to use one source as the primary message and the other as supplementary? Do both need to be considered as comparable in importance, and dissonances resolved? Do we finesse the issue by thinking of them as means of answering different subquestions?

The field of evaluation may be growing toward a third paradigm. Questions about mixed methods are becoming well stated. As the 1992 American Evaluation Association meeting demonstrated, the number of well-reported experiences with mixed models on which firmer theory and practice can develop is rapidly expanding. And there is a sense of readiness to see the world as a scuba diver might, going beyond hook and net. This third paradigm, one that I think of as adaptive evaluation, perhaps similar to what House (this volume) calls realistic evaluation, derives its worldview from what is required to reflect adequately the imperatives of decisions and the complexities of the environments in which action and policy occur. Its theoretical basis and vision have yet to be articulated as eloquently as Guba and Lincoln (1989) or as forcefully as Rossi and Freeman (1993). I believe, however, that someday this third paradigm will find its voice and, for a while, will unite us.

References

Berk, R. A., and others. "Social Policy Experimentation: A Policy Paper." Evaluation Review, 1985, 399–403.

Boruch, R. F. "Comparative Aspects of Randomized Experiments for Planning and Evaluation." In M. Bulmer (ed.), Social Science and Government: Comparative Essays on Britain and the United States. Cambridge, England: Cambridge University Press, 1987.

Campbell, D. T. "Qualitative Knowing in Action Research." Kurt Lewin Award address presented at the annual meeting of the American Psychological Association, New Orleans, La., Sept. 1974.

Campbell, D. T., and Fiske, D. W. "Convergent and Discriminant Validation by the Multitrait-Multimethod Matrix." Psychological Bulletin, 1959, 56, 81–105.

Cook, T. D., and Reichardt, C. S. (eds.). Qualitative and Quantitative Methods in Evaluation Research. Newbury Park, Calif.: Sage, 1979.

Datta, L. "Strange Bedfellows." American Behavioral Scientist, 1982, 26 (1), 133–144.

Datta, L. Case Study Evaluations. Transfer Paper 10.1.9. Washington, D.C.: General Accounting Office, 1990.

Denny, T. "Some Still Do: River Acres, Texas." Unpublished manuscript, n.d.

Farley, J. "Combining Quantitative and Qualitative Methods in Evaluation Research." State Evaluation Network Newsletter, 1981, 1, 3–5.

Fetterman, D. M. "Ethnography and Policy: A Catalytic Combination for Change." Unpublished manuscript, Stanford University, n.d.

Fetterman, D. M. "Gifted and Talented Education: A National Test Case in Peoria." Educational Evaluation and Policy Analysis, 1986, 8 (2), 155–166.

Fetterman, D. M. Excellence and Equality: A Qualitatively Different Perspective on Gifted and Talented Education. Albany: State University of New York Press, 1988.

Fetterman, D. M. "In Response to Lee Sechrest's 1991 AEA Presidential Address: 'Roots: Back to Our First Generations,' February 1991, 1–7." Evaluation Practice, 1992, 13, 171–172.

Fetterman, D. M., and Pitman, M. A. Educational Evaluation: Ethnography in Theory, Practice, and Politics. Newbury Park, Calif.: Sage, 1986.

General Accounting Office. Federal Evaluation: Fewer Units, Reduced Resources, Different Studies from 1980. PEMD-87–9. Washington, D.C.: General Accounting Office, 1987.

General Accounting Office. Illegal Aliens: Influence of Illegal Workers on Wages and Working Conditions of Legal Workers. PEMD-88–13BR. Washington, D.C.: General Accounting Office, 1988.

Goetz, J. P., and LeCompte, M. D. "Ethnographic Research and the Problem of Data Reduction." Anthropology and Education Quarterly, 1981, 12, 51–70.

Greenberg, D., and Shroder, M. Digest of the Social Experiments. Special Report No. 52. Madison: Institute for Research on Poverty, University of Wisconsin, 1991.

Greene, J. C., Caracelli, V. J., and Graham, W. F. "Toward a Conceptual Framework for Mixed-Method Evaluation Designs." Educational Evaluation and Policy Analysis, 1989, 11 (3), 255–274.

Guba, E. G. "Criteria for Assessing the Trustworthiness of Naturalistic Inquiry." Education, Communication, and Technology Journal, 1981, 8, 42–54.

Guba, E. G., and Lincoln, Y. S. Fourth-Generation Evaluation. Newbury Park, Calif.: Sage, 1989.

Halpern, E. S. "Auditing Naturalistic Inquiries: Some Preliminary Applications." Paper presented at the annual meeting of the American Educational Research Association, Toronto, Ontario, Canada, Apr. 1983.

Heckman, J. J. Randomization and Social Policy Evaluation. Technical Working Paper No. 107. Cambridge, Mass.: National Bureau of Economic Research, 1991.

Hedges, L. V., and Olkin, I. Statistical Methods for Meta-Analysis. San Diego: Academic Press, 1985.

Henze, R. Case Study of a Bilingual/Bicultural Program, Kwigillingok, October 17–20, 1989. Oakland, Calif.: ARC Associates, 1990a.

Henze, R. An Exploratory Study of the Effectiveness of the Lower Kuskokwin School District's Bilingual Program. Oakland, Calif.: ARC Associates, 1990b.

Jick, T. D. "Mixing Qualitative and Quantitative Methods: Triangulation in Action." Administrative Science Quarterly, 1979, 24, 602–611.

Levitan, S. A. Evaluation of Federal Social Programs: An Uncertain Impact. Occasional Paper 1992–2. Washington, D.C.: Center for Social Policy Studies, 1992.

Lincoln, Y. S. "Strategies for Inquiring About the Dependability (Reliability) of Naturalistic Studies." Paper presented at the annual meeting of the Evaluation Research Society, Austin, Tex., Sept.-Oct. 1981.

Lincoln, Y. S. "The Arts and Sciences of Program Evaluation." Evaluation Practice, 1991, 12 (1), 1–7.

Louis, K. S. "Policy Researcher as Sleuth: New Approaches to Integrating Qualitative and Quantitative Methods." Paper presented at the annual meeting of the American Educational Research Association, Los Angeles, Apr. 1981. (ED 207 256)

Madey, D. L. "Some Benefits of Integrating Qualitative and Quantitative Methods in Program Evaluation, with Illustrations." Educational Evaluation and Policy Analysis, 1982, 4, 223–236.

Mark, M. M., and Shotland, R. L. (eds.). Multiple Methods in Program Evaluation. New Directions for Program Evaluation, no. 35. San Francisco: Jossey-Bass, 1987.

Martin, G. O. "The Uses of Qualitative and Quantitative Methods for Program Evaluation. The California International Studies Project: A Case Study." Paper presented at the annual meeting of the American Evaluation Association, Boston, Oct. 1987.

Meyers, S. K. "Occupational Therapy Treatment of an Adult with an Eating Disorder: One Woman's Experience." Occupational Therapy in Mental Health, 1989a, 9 (1), 33–47.

Meyers, S. K. "Program Evaluation of Occupational Therapy Level II Fieldwork Environments: A Naturalistic Inquiry." Occupational Therapy Journal of Research, 1989b, 9 (6), 357–361.

Miles, M. B., and Huberman, M. Qualitative Data Analysis: A Sourcebook of New Methods. Newbury Park, Calif.: Sage, 1984.

Miles, M. B., and Huberman, M. "Some Procedures for Causal Analysis of Multiple-Case Data." Qualitative Studies in Education, 1989, 2 (1), 55–68.

Patton, M. Q. Qualitative Evaluation Methods. Newbury Park, Calif.: Sage, 1980.

Patton, M. Q. How to Use Qualitative Methods in Evaluation. Newbury Park, Calif.: Sage, 1987.

Reed, M. C. "A Critique of Fourth-Generation Evaluation." Paper presented at the annual meeting of the American Evaluation Association, Chicago, Oct. 1991.

Regan, K. Case Study of a Yupik First Language/Dual Program, Kasigluk, Alaska, October 24–27, 1989. Oakland, Calif.: ARC Associates, 1990.

Rist, R. C. "On the Relations Between Educational Research Paradigms: From Disdain to Detente." Anthropology and Education Quarterly, 1972, 8, 42–49.

Rossi, P. H., and Freeman, H. E. Evaluation: A Systematic Approach. (5th ed.) Newbury Park, Calif.: Sage, 1993.

R.O.W. Sciences and Institute for Public Policy Studies. Final Evaluation Plan. Contract No. ADM 281–90–0003. Nashville, Tenn.: Institute for Policy Studies, Vanderbilt University, 1991.

Sechrest, L. "Roots: Back to Our First Generations." Evaluation Practice, 1992, 13 (1), 1–7.

Sieber, S. "Integration of Fieldwork and Survey Methods." American Journal of Sociology, 1973, 78, 1335–1359.

Smith, A. G., and Louis, K. S. (eds.). Multimethod Policy Research: Issues and Applications. Special issue of American Behavioral Scientist, 1982, 26 (entire issue 1).

Smith, J. K. "Quantitative Versus Qualitative Research: An Attempt to Clarify the Issue." Educational Researcher, 1983, 12 (3), 6–13.

Smith, J. K., and Heshusius, L. "Closing Down the Conversation: The End of the Quantitative-Qualitative Debate Among Educational Inquirers." Educational Researcher, 1986, 15 (1), 4–12.

Smith, M. L. "The Whole Is Greater: Combining Qualitative and Quantitative Approaches in Evaluation Studies." In D. D. Williams (ed.), Naturalistic Evaluation. New Directions for Program Evaluation, no. 30. San Francisco: Jossey-Bass, 1986.

Trend, M. J. "On the Reconciliation of Qualitative and Quantitative Analyses: A Case Study." In T. D. Cook and C. S. Reichardt (eds.), Qualitative and Quantitative Methods in Evaluation Research. Newbury Park, Calif.: Sage, 1979.

Vanett, L. Case Study of Yupik as a Second Language Program, Bethel, November 26–December 1, 1989. Oakland, Calif.: ARC Associates, 1990.

Wax, R. H. Doing Fieldwork: Warnings and Advice. Chicago: University of Chicago Press, 1971.

Weiss, C. H. "Politics and Evaluation: A Reprise in Mellower Overtones." Evaluation Practice, 1993, 14 (1), 107–109.

Wolf, R. L. Final Report: Studying School Governance Through Judicial Evaluation Procedures. Report to the Lilly Endowment. Bloomington: Center for Evaluation, Indiana University, 1978.

Wolf, R. L., and Tymitz, B. L. When Will the Fourth Floor Be Open? A Study of Visitor Perceptions of the Hirschorn Museum and Sculpture Garden, Smithsonian Institution. Washington, D.C.: Museum Evaluation Studies Program, Smithsonian Institution, 1980.

Wolf, R. L., and Tymitz, B. L. Hey Mom, That Exhibit's Alive: A Study of Visitor Perceptions of the Coral Reef Exhibit, National Museum of Natural History. Washington, D.C.: Museum Evaluation Studies Program, Smithsonian Institution, 1981.

Yin, R. K. Case Study Research: Design and Methods. (3rd ed.) Newbury Park, Calif.: Sage, 1989.

LOIS-ELLIN DATTA is president of Datta Analysis, Waikoloa, Hawaii. She formerly worked for the U.S. General Accounting Office, the U.S. Department of Education, and the Office of Economic Opportunity and is past president of the Evaluation Research Society.

This chapter identifies four commonalities between qualitative and
quantitative research, thereby creating a new synthesis to diminish the
divisiveness between the two camps.

Evaluation: A Singular Craft

Robert K. Yin

This chapter departs from my normal theme. Usually, I present concepts and practical applications of the case study method (Yin, 1989). However, the editors of this volume posed a different challenge. They asked me to address the exchange of views by two past presidents of the American Evaluation Association (AEA) (Lincoln, 1991; Sechrest, 1992) and to reflect on whether we share commonalities in evaluation and, if so, what they might be.

Is There Common Ground?

The exchange of AEA presidential views in 1991 and 1992 reflects the division in evaluation practice between research that is alternatively qualitative versus quantitative, logical versus intuitive, subjective versus objective, and so on. I need not review here how the lines of division also have been exacerbated by activities within AEA, by *Fourth-Generation Evaluation* (Guba and Lincoln, 1989), and by the ensuing counterexchange of yet other views (Reed, 1991; Fetterman, 1992). Rather than reinforce these conflicts by analyzing them further, I instead chose to point constructively at the essential characteristics of the evaluation craft. These are the characteristics that we share in common and the concepts that we must share as the foundation of the evaluation craft.

This chapter was conceived at a time when I happened to be reading two pertinent books: William Bennett's (1992) *The De-Valuing of America: The Fight*

I thank David Cordray (president of AEA during 1991–1992), Richard Light (Harvard University), 1992 AEA program co-chairs Charles Reichardt (University of Denver) and Sharon Rallis (Regional Laboratory for Educational Improvement of the Northeast and Islands), Fred Mosteller, and Graham Allison for their input.

for Our Culture and Our Children and Arthur M. Schlesinger, Jr.'s (1991) The Disuniting of America: Reflections on a Multicultural Society. Both books focus on cultural conflicts—possibly analogous to conflicts reflected in the presidential exchange on evaluation. Bennett depicted himself as a fighter and fighting as the only means of gaining the upper hand. His pugnacious nature is reflected by such comments as "some of my critics may be able to look forward to having Bill Bennett to kick around some more. Fair enough. I promise to kick back" (p. 252). He has attacked his challengers as if they were part of "a struggle of fighting faiths" (p. 228). Likewise, Schlesinger has dealt with the problem of ethnic identities. Within this problem, contemporary American ethnic and racial groups have been using history as "therapy," as Schlesinger calls it. He views this as a corruption of the use of history, also leading to too great an emphasis on pluribus and leaving little attention to unum.

These and other writings and events do suggest that conflict—deep, culturally based, generationally based, unremitting conflict—may be in the scholarly air. However, I personally do not subscribe to this orientation. For me, the greater challenge is to create new syntheses to establish a common ground. In this spirit, I therefore attempt here to extract and reiterate the commonalities found in diverse, classic, social science research, purposefully choosing to represent the archetypical quantitative, qualitative, and experimental modes of doing research.

Two classic studies represent exemplary quantitative or qualitative research: Mosteller and Wallace's (1984) Applied Bayesian and Classical Inference and Allison's (1971) Essence of Decision. In addition, I use my own work in experimental psychology (Yin, 1969, 1970a, 1970b, 1978) as a further comparison, not because it is classic but because it represents normative experimental behavioral science. The two classic works and my research are reviewed from the standpoint of their basic research logics. My claim is that these logics are similar, and that this is the common ground we share. (I did not choose evaluation studies as illustrations because they are covered by Datta, this volume.)

Mosteller and Wallace, 1984

This is the second edition of a book first published in 1964. The book contains extensive analysis and the application of Bayes's theorem to determine the odds of authorship for disputed papers. The book is regarded as a classic in statistics and is therefore used here to illustrate quantitative research.

Disputed Authorship: *The Federalist* **Papers.** The documents in dispute were twelve of the seventy-seven Federalist papers published during the period 1787–1788. These papers were mainly authored by Alexander Hamilton, James Madison, and John Jay, although each paper was signed anonymously by "Publius." The papers are of significant importance in American history and are now considered part of our national heritage. Their specific purpose at that time was to persuade the citizens of New York State to ratify the U.S. Constitution. The papers range from 900 to 3,500 words.

Of the seventy-seven papers, forty-three are known to have been authored by Hamilton, fourteen by Madison, five by Jay, and three by both Hamilton and Madison. Sole authorship of the remaining twelve papers was subsequently claimed by both Hamilton and Madison. Historians have not definitively settled the dispute, differing over time in the crediting of authorship. During the nineteenth century, most historians favored Hamilton; whereas during the twentieth century, historians have favored Madison. Mosteller and Wallace's analysis provides compelling evidence that the author of all of the disputed papers was Madison.

Analytical Strategies. Settlement of the dispute has been a difficult matter. Because each author was writing as an advocate and not necessarily representing his own views, political context and consistency with previous writings could not be readily used to reach a conclusion. Mosteller and Wallace's alternative approach was to compare the pattern of word usage in the disputed papers with that found in the papers whose authorship is known. However, such comparisons also proved difficult because Hamilton and Madison wrote in similar styles.

For instance, Mosteller, as part of a preliminary inquiry in the early 1940s with a co-worker in graduate school, counted the number of words for each sentence in those papers whose authorship was known. The results are shown in Table 7.1. Not only were the authors very similar, the sentences were long, reflecting the style admired in the colonial period: formal and complicated, with long words, and crowded with qualifications. In Mosteller and Wallace's words, "You will observe that the sentence length is long . . . and that the large standard deviation means that some sentences were very long" (p. 7). As another example, the earlier inquiry also investigated the proportion of nouns, adjectives, and short words in the papers. Although Hamilton and Madison did differ here and a pattern was suggested, the evidence was not sufficiently strong to resolve the dispute. At that point, no further research took place.

About fifteen years later, a historian informed Mosteller that he had found a pair of words that readily distinguished the writings of Hamilton and Madison: Hamilton used while, whereas in similar situations Madison used whilst. Mosteller called these "marker" words and set upon identifying other marker words—where one author used the words frequently and the other rarely. It is noteworthy that contextual words were rejected as useful marker words because contextual words vary greatly with the topic of a paper. Thus, the candidate marker words were all noncontextual (see Exhibit 7.1).

Table 7.1. Results of Handcounting Words in The Federalist Papers

Author	Average Length of Sentence	Standard Deviation
Hamilton	34.55 words	19.2
Madison	34.59 words	20.3

**Exhibit 7.1. Illustrative List of Noncontextual Words
in The Federalist Papers**

According
Also
Although
Always
An
Apt
Both
By
Commonly
Consequently
Considerable(ly)
Direction
Enough
Innovation(s)
Kind
Language
Matter(s)
Of
On
Particularly
Probability
There
This
Though
To
Upon
Vigor(ous)
While
Whilst
Work(s)

The identification of the marker words led to the ultimate design and conduct of the main study reported in Mosteller and Wallace (1984). Of 165 words originally identified, 30 were used in the main study. The study's goals were to settle the authorship of each of the disputed papers, on an individual basis, and not just as a group; use many marker words, to increase the stability of the findings; construct an acceptable probability model to represent the variability in word rate from paper to paper; and therefore assess the likelihood of authorship in probabilistic terms. To further stabilize the results, because Madison only authored fourteen Federalist papers, his sample of writings was expanded to include thirty-six additional writings, to create a broader data base (Mosteller and Wallace, 1984, p. 19). The investigators favored the use of Bayesian statistics because this application represented an ideal opportunity to show how Bayes's theorem could be applied to a real-life situation.

Conclusions. The book presents detailed operational steps on the procedures for dividing the papers into two-hundred-word blocks and developing the mathematical models needed to establish the needed probabilities. The result was that for most of the papers the odds were on average sixty thousand to one in favor of Madison (p. 88). The two weakest odds were for Paper 55 (ninety to one in favor of Madison) and Paper 56 (eight hundred to one in favor of Madison) (p. 263). As a result, the investigators concluded that Madison was the author of all twelve disputed papers.

Allison, 1971

This book was the result of about eight years of intensive study and has undergone numerous reprintings. The book is now acknowledged as a classic in contemporary political science and is widely used in university courses everywhere. It is therefore used as my example of qualitative research.

The Cuban Missile Crisis. During thirteen days in October 1962—from Tuesday, October 16, through Sunday, October 28—the United States and the former Soviet Union stood closer to nuclear holocaust than any other two countries in all of history. As described by Allison, "The United States and the Soviet Union stood 'eyeball to eyeball,' each with the power of annihilation in hand. The United States was firm but forebearing. The Soviet Union looked hard, blinked twice, and then withdrew without humiliation. Here is one of the finest examples of diplomatic prudence, and perhaps the finest hour of John F. Kennedy's Presidency" (p. 39). Only three years earlier, Cuba had been taken over by Fidel Castro—at first a hero within the United States but soon after a surprising devotee of communism. President Kennedy (JFK) had already tried unsuccessfully to dislodge Castro in the spring of 1961 (the Bay of Pigs). Then, despite Soviet assurances to the contrary during September 1962, the United States detected the placement of Soviet offensive missiles in Cuba. So began the Cuban missile crisis.

The United States learned of the missiles' existence on Tuesday, October 16, as a result of a U-2 overflight. However, this knowledge was only divulged publicly six days later (Monday, October 22), when JFK announced the discovery and also proclaimed that the United States would put a naval quarantine (blockade) into place. He also demanded that the Soviet Union halt its massive buildup, which included the offensive, ground-to-ground intermediate range ballistic missiles.

The quarantine was to take effect on Wednesday, October 24. The procedures called for U.S. forces to stop any Soviet ship approaching Cuba, board it, and prevent any missile-related supplies from proceeding to Cuba. On Friday, October 26, the U.S. Navy actually boarded a Soviet ship trying to avoid the quarantine. The ship was eventually allowed to pass. Two days later, despite U.S. worries that the quarantine was not working well, Soviet prime minister Nikita Khruschev announced that the Soviets would dismantle the missiles and return them to the Soviet Union. The crisis was over.

Analytical Questions. In reviewing the events that took place, Allison identified three essential questions about the Cuban missile crisis: Why had the Soviets placed offensive missiles in Cuba in the first place? Why had the United States responded with a naval quarantine, given that the first batch of missiles was already in place? Why did the Soviets withdraw, given that the quarantine was a strange response and also was not working with complete effectiveness? To answer these questions, Allison called on the rival explanations put forth by three major theoretical positions within social science: "great man" or rational actor theory, organizational process theory, and political process theory.

Analytical Strategies. Allison applied the three theories to the events of the crisis, pattern matching the actual course of events with the conditions considered important to each (rival) theory. The rational actor theory assumes that events are a result of singular decision making, oriented solely at the problem at hand. The organizational process theory assumes that bureaucratic organizations are involved in all decision making, and that routine bureaucratic processes (unknowingly) affect the end results. The political process theory assumes that actions are the result of negotiations, compromises, and conflicts among individuals within their respective governments. All three theories are major theories within Allison's field, emanating from the works of esteemed scholars such as Hans Morgenthau, Thomas Schelling, and Robert McNamara (rational actor); James March and Herbert Simon (organizational process); and Richard Neustadt, Gabriel Almond, and Charles Lindblom (political process).

For instance, brief repetition of the facts just presented reveals the illogical nature of the sequence of the events from the rational actor standpoint. First, the theory might account for the Soviets' placement of the offensive missiles as an act of Cold War politics, even though the Soviets had been issuing contrary assurances to the United States throughout September 1962 and earlier, and the United States had clearly warned the Soviets that "the introduction of offensive missiles into Cuba would raise the gravest issue" (p. 40). However, the more logical responses by the United States would have been a surgical air strike or even a full-scale invasion of Cuba, but not a naval quarantine, because the missiles were already in Cuba. Further, the theory would have difficulty explaining why the Soviets camouflaged the missiles after the United States announced their discovery, not before. Even further, the theory cannot explain why the missiles were installed prior to the installation of surface-to-air missiles, known to be effective in shooting down U-2s. Finally, the theory also would have trouble explaining why withdrawal came twenty-four hours after the United States' "blackest day of the crisis" (October 27), when (1) a Soviet ship had detached itself from the others and appeared to be testing the blockade, (2) the completion of the missile sites in Cuba continued at an even more feverish pace, and (3) the surface-to-air missiles were finally operational and had shot down a U-2 plane over Cuba. Allison's major analysis therefore consists of the repeated recitation of the facts of the Cuban missile crisis, showing how the facts might fit each rival theory.

Conclusions. After explicitly matching the facts of the missile crisis to the patterns predicted by each of the theories in turn, Allison concluded that the organizational process and political process theories both offer important insights into government action, even though the rational actor theory has dominated our thinking in the past.

Example from Experimental Psychology—Yin, 1969, 1970a, 1970b

Neither of the preceding studies actually involved an experimental treatment or intervention. As a result, my own research in experimental psychology rounds out the collection of studies.

How People Recognize Faces. The problem addressed was how people can readily and quickly recognize hundreds of faces, even though from any objective standpoint the faces represent highly similar visual patterns (Yin, 1970a). This capability raises the possibility that different social and even physiological processes might be involved in face recognition, compared to those processes used to recognize regular visual patterns. Important evidence for such different processes might come by comparing the performance of normal adults on face recognition with performance on other visual recognition tasks. More intriguing evidence might come by similarly comparing the performances of normal and brain-injured adults whose injuries were localizable to critical parts of the brain.

This investigation came at a time when rapid advances were being made in our understanding of the visual recognition of complex objects, stemming both from discoveries in physiological psychology and from development of computer capabilities. Despite these advances, however, few investigations had previously addressed the specific problem of how people recognize faces— surely one of the most important of all human visual functions.

Analytical Strategies. The main analytical strategy took advantage of a well-known phenomenon: Upside-down faces are extremely difficult to recognize. Based on this phenomenon, I created a series of experiments that compared visual recognition performance when (1) faces were presented rightside up, (2) faces were presented upside down, (3) other classes of complex, "mono-oriented" visual objects (such as pictures of houses) were presented rightside up, and (4) these other classes were presented upside down. Individuals were asked to view a series of pictures (for example, twenty pictures of faces and twenty pictures of houses) and then were tested to see how many pictures they could recognize in a subsequent trial (Yin, 1969, 1970b). To analyze the data, analysis of variance and accompanying F and t tests were used. The analysis of variance ensured that all main, interactive, and simple effects were investigated in a quantitatively precise manner.

Other experiments did not necessarily turn faces upside down but instead tested memory for these different types of objects under alternative conditions. For instance, one test was for a person to write a brief description of individual face and house pictures, and then to match these descriptions back to the pictures a week later. This kind of test not only provided more information about performance but also yielded clues regarding useful recognition strategies (Yin, 1970a).

Conclusions. Under every condition, face recognition performance differed from the recognition of other complex, visual objects. People's exceptional performance in recognizing faces was not attributable to their performance in recognizing other objects. The possibility of their using a special code for face recognition was supported by their difficulties in recognizing faces under certain conditions of distortion, for example, inversion of the faces, when the code cannot be used and when face recognition is therefore poorer than the recognition of other objects; or under certain conditions of brain injury, for example, when the injury is in the right posterior part of the brain.

Commonalities Among the Studies

These three studies were selected to reflect wide-ranging differences in methods, concepts, and academic fields. Despite these differences, the studies share important commonalities. The commonalities may serve as the beginning of a unified foundation for evaluation research. Four such commonalities are discussed next.

Thorough Coverage and Investigation of All Evidence. The two classic studies presented evidence thoroughly, leaving the impression that any other evidence also would have been welcomed and examined. The overall impression is that few others would be likely to present additional evidence that might challenge the original studies (except for some new event, such as the release of archival evidence from the Soviets in the case of Allison's study).

In his preliminary inquiry, Mosteller and his co-worker counted every word in every sentence in The Federalist papers. Their "first frustration," noted later by Mosteller and Wallace (1984, p. 7), was "the discovery of an important empirical principle—people cannot count, at least not very high." A second difficulty was the need to establish certain rules: How should quotations from other authors be handled? How should numbers written out or in numerals be counted in words, and so on? In the main study, the augmenting of the evidentiary base by adding extra Madison papers and investigating a large number of marker words reflects a penchant for thoroughness. On all counts, the investigators could have settled for less evidence.

Allison's (1971) work is unabashedly and impressively exhaustive. Even though the amount of information in public, primary sources was "extraordinary" (p. viii), his study was based on all information in the published record, interviews with most of the high-level participants in the crisis, and interviews with a large number of people in the lower-level operations of the U.S. government. Further, Allison acknowledged the shortage of evidence from the Soviet side but worked with everything that was made available.

The face recognition example does not offer as impressive a record, although it consists of six separate experiments. Two of these also entailed additional comparison conditions to augment the main experiment, thereby creating a total of eight experiments. Further, five different series of face pictures and five different series of mono-oriented objects were used throughout these experiments to ensure that the results were based on a diverse evidentiary base.

Constant Awareness and Testing of Rival Hypotheses. A second commonality among the studies is a constant awareness of rival hypotheses, including those resulting from methodological artifacts, leaving the impression that no plausible counterargument was ignored. Mosteller and Wallace started with their main rival hypotheses—that either Madison or Hamilton was the author of the disputed papers. But they also entertained other possibilities. One was that some other person, most likely John Jay, was the author; this possibility was tested and rejected (p. 248). Another, more subtle possibility was that Madison edited what was originally a Hamilton paper. Although this could not be definitively ruled out, Madison "would have had to remove about 50 occurrences of Hamilton words among the final 30, and to add about 20 occurrences of Madison words" (p. 90). Further, he would have had to do this with all twelve papers, and he would have had to know the thirty marker words that Mosteller and Wallace would be using two hundred years later (p. 264). Again, had only a few marker words been used, this remote possibility would have been much more likely.

However, the most impressive rival hypotheses entertained by Mosteller and Wallace are related to potential artifacts. In separate chapters, the authors conducted three additional studies, each using a different methodology, demonstrating that the results of the main study were not dependent on parametric assumptions and heavy, automated calculations (robust, hand-calculated Bayesian analysis), effects of outliers in distorting the main results (three-category analysis), or use of Bayes's theorem (weight-rate analysis, using a more traditional approach to problems of discrimination).

In a similar manner, Allison's entire study is based on the testing of rival hypotheses—in his case, the distinctions among the three theories. One important result of this testing is the conclusion that JFK's threat to take further action—an ultimatum—and not just the quarantine alone actually led to the withdrawal of the missiles (pp. 64 and 218). As Allison noted, "Most previous . . . analyses have accepted the blockade as a satisfactory base for building an explanation of the Soviet withdrawal. . . . Ours is the first published account to emphasize the U.S. ultimatum to the Soviet Union as the central factor in the Soviet withdrawal" (p. 247). Similarly, the use of the rival hypotheses permitted Allison, in his final explanation of events, to put into perspective many other details of the missile crisis.

Rival hypotheses were at the heart of my face recognition studies, too. The whole series of studies was devoted to a comparison of face pictures with pictures of other objects to ensure that performance on face recognition tasks could not be accounted for by performance on picture recognition more generally. A more subtle rival hypothesis had to do with the potential artifactual effects of the shading in face pictures, the possibility being that shaded objects are grossly distorted when inverted, thereby accounting for the deteriorated performance under that condition. To test this rival, one of the six experiments used line drawings of faces and of other objects to replicate the results of the other experiments.

Yet other rival hypotheses were related to the findings with brain-injured adults. The people tested in this experiment included sufficient numbers of persons with injuries in multiple cortical locations (left and right, posterior and frontal, and bilateral), closed head injuries (no penetrating wound), and normal controls—all to test the conclusion regarding the deficient performance by those with injuries to the right posterior portions of their brains.

Finally, the study implicitly addressed another common methodological rival in experimental psychology, that statistically significant results have been produced only because of the use of large sample sizes (hundreds or even thousands of data points). In such situations, the results are not considered phenomenologically important from a psychological standpoint. For this reason, significant effects are even more valued if they are obtained with small samples of subjects (see Table 7.2).

Results with Significant Implications. A third commonality is that the results of these studies all potentially had significant implications beyond the immediate work. In concluding their study, Mosteller and Wallace devoted an entire chapter to the problems of disputed authorship and how these disputes have been investigated. Many of the examples are of great significance in Western literary tradition: the controversy over the writings of William Shakespeare and Sir Francis Bacon, the accusations of Mikhail Sholokhov's plagiarism in And Quiet Flows the Don, a book on ethics reputedly authored by Aristotle, and the Bible. The discussion also covers legal disputes, where evidence about authorship has been a critical part of trials and their dispositions.

Table 7.2. Number of Subjects and Significance Levels in Face Recognition Experiments

Experiment	Number of Subjects	Statistical Level of Significance for Main Effects
1	26	$p < .001$
2	21	$p < .01$
3	23	$p < .001$
4	22	$p < .01$
5	34	$p < .001$
6	68	$p < .002$

Note: All subjects were normal adults except in Experiment 6, which involved thirty-seven people with penetrating brain injuries, nineteen people with closed head injuries, and twelve normal controls.

Mosteller and Wallace also contributed significantly to the development of statistical methods. Mosteller (personal communication, June 17, 1992) wrote modestly that they used "a lot of methods that later became well-known."

Allison intended his work to generalize to other international confrontations and even other public policy controversies not embedded in international or military affairs. Among the international confrontations cited are President Johnson's decision to bomb North Vietnam, the U.S. involvement in Vietnam more generally, and NATO's defense problems. Among the domestic topics are the politics of Medicare.

Finally, the face recognition results were intended to enlighten the entire topic of how human beings sustain meaningful interpersonal relationships. Related work includes a large number of experiments on infants' recognition of faces, an occult study in reading the character of faces (physiognomy), and a rare clinical syndrome in which a person cannot recognize faces of personally familiar persons, including one's own mirror image (prosopagnosia).

Investigatory Expertise About the Subject. A fourth commonality is derived by inference. The investigators demonstrated a depth of expertise about the subject matter, reflected by a penchant for details, extensive side commentary, and other supplemental information. The overall (subjective) impression is that each investigator knew much more about the subject matter than was included in the final study.

Mosteller and Wallace's book contains not only the main study and the additional methodological studies cited above but also a whole chapter on the theoretical basis of the main study: "In a textbook, [this chapter] would be starred; the chapters that follow are not dependent on the material in this chapter, and most readers would do well to skip it on first reading. Unlike the other chapters, this chapter is written only for those seriously interested in statistical theory" (p. 92). The chapter then elucidates the properties of the negative binomial distribution, a key data distribution used in the main study; properties of the Poisson distribution, also used in the main study; issues surrounding the calculation of the logarithmic odds used in the main study; and other related topics. The chapter contains numerous equations and calculations. Moreover, this single chapter, one of ten chapters in the entire book, comprises one hundred pages of the three-hundred-page book. This indeed symbolizes the investigators' expertise in the subject matter.

Allison's book shares the same characteristic of expertise, best reflected in the quantity and quality of his book's footnotes. They run a full 50 small-print pages, more than the original text of 275 pages. They read with great care and precision, clarifying subtle issues in the text, key sources, methodological assumptions made by the author, potential gaps or conflicts in the evidence, and additional background information. As one might suspect, to the specialist in the field (similar to the serious student of statistical theory), these footnotes are a gold mine of information and offer interesting reading in their own right.

Similarly, the face recognition work reported in Yin (1978) includes an exhaustive review of the literature, covering most of the pertinent experimental evidence presented during the twentieth century. However, in all fairness, no claim is made that the study reflects the same degree of investigatory expertise as those of the two classics.

Summary: Defining the Common Ground. These four characteristics begin to define our common ground as evaluators. My claim is that the practices of detailing evidence, thinking about rival explanations, seeking results with significant implications, and demonstrating investigatory expertise in the subject matter are found in all good evaluations, whether the evaluations are qualitative or quantitative, first generation or fourth generation, and so on. Conversely, we are most dissatisfied with our work when these four characteristics are jeopardized, for instance, when our evaluations force us to limit our evidence, to avoid recognizing rival explanations, to focus inwardly on issues of minor importance, or to become instant experts on a subject.

Further, the four characteristics are not simply a product of the three illustrative studies selected. They also can be found in such diverse methodological texts as Barzun and Graff's (1985) The Modern Researcher, Kidder and Judd's (1986) Research Methods in Social Relations, and John Van Maanen's (1988) Tales of the Field: On Writing Ethnography. Stereotypically, these books might be seen to cover methods in history, quantitative studies, and ethnography. The first two have been so widely used that they are in their fourth and fifth editions, respectively, with roughly thirty years or more of published history since the first editions. Van Maanen's book is comparatively recent but is a remarkable contribution to ethnographic methodology. Although he thinks that his book is about ethnographic writing, in actuality the book also is about research designs in ethnography.

Examination of these three books from the perspective of the four common characteristics reveals the following. First, from the perspective of detailing evidence, all three books present different terminologies and different types of evidence, but notions of thoroughness and investigatory evidence are pervasive in the problem of defining a historical "fact," the desire for converging quantitative data, and ethnographic "thick description." Second, rival explanations also are discussed, though again in different ways: truth and causation and the role of patterns in history, rival hypotheses and research designs in quantitative research, and alternative types of tales in ethnography. Third, the books are all oriented toward research whose results have significant implications: history as the treatment of "a large slice of the past" in lasting fashion, social relations as the study of how people behave with and toward others, and ethnography as the study of culture, to conceptualize, reflect, narrate, and evaluate it. Finally, all of the books challenge the reader to become serious scholars and demonstrate investigatory expertise: the importance of verification techniques in history, the maximizing of construct, internal, and external validity in quantitative studies, and the intensity of fieldwork and use of participant observation in ethnography.

In sum, the commonalities transcend the differences. In fact, the commonalities help us to rediscover that evaluation is not a debate between doing science and doing art but rather a craft that falls within the same single rubric: social science.

Work That Lies Ahead

Identifying and describing the commonalities is but a first step. This chapter is but a partial beginning of this step. The step may be subject to modification, and additional commonalities also may be added. However, evaluators should not await the completion of this first step before starting the next steps. The next steps are to begin sharing these commonalities, to bring into our methodological vocabulary, and to market our work to clients so that they know the importance of these commonalities in the production of good evaluations. In fact, one benchmark for the success of this venture is to test how clients think about evaluations. Currently, the qualitative and quantitative differences have seeped undesirably into the clients' perceptual world. For instance, because of the evaluators' debate, clients who have little or no social science training are now asking about the differences among ethnography, fieldwork, grounded theory, case studies, surveys, and the like. The clients are commissioning evaluation studies that appear to combine two or more of these methods, sometimes in ways that do not fit. I do not think that this kind of client involvement in methodological subtleties is healthy. Evaluators hardly know how to describe the differences or combine the methods. Instead, I would be satisfied if clients were hounding evaluators (or issuing requests for proposals) on the following points:

- Insisting on complete and thorough evidence (but leaving the definition of evidence to the evaluators)
- Welcoming the development of rival ideas
- Demanding that the evaluation findings have significant implications
- Ensuring that evaluators bring a breadth of knowledge, based on a record of persistent previous inquiry, to the topic being evaluated

When this happens, our work in establishing a common ground will have begun to succeed.

References

Allison, G. T. Essence of Decision: Explaining the Cuban Missile Crisis. Boston: Little, Brown, 1971.

Barzun, J., and Graff, H. F. The Modern Researcher. (4th ed.) Orlando, Fla.: Harcourt Brace Jovanovich, 1985.

Bennett, W. J. The De-Valuing of America: The Fight for Our Culture and Our Children. New York: Summit Books, 1992.

Fetterman, D. M. "In Response to Lee Sechrest's 1991 AEA Presidential Address: 'Roots: Back to Our First Generations,' February 1991, 1–7." Evaluation Practice, 1992, 13, 171–172.

Guba, E., and Lincoln, Y. Fourth-Generation Evaluation. Newbury Park, Calif.: Sage, 1989.

Kidder, L. H., and Judd, C. M. Research Methods in Social Relations. (5th ed.) Troy, Mo.: Holt, Rinehart & Winston, 1986.

Lincoln, Y. S. "The Arts and Sciences of Program Evaluation." Evaluation Practice, 1991, 12 (1), 1–7.

Mosteller, F., and Wallace, D. L. Applied Bayesian and Classical Inference: The Case of "The Federalist" Papers. (2nd ed.) New York: Springer-Verlag, 1984.

Reed, M. C. "A Critique of Fourth-Generation Evaluation." Paper presented at the annual meeting of the American Evaluation Association, Chicago, Oct. 1991.

Schlesinger, A. M., Jr. The Disuniting of America: Reflections on a Multicultural Society. New York: Norton, 1991.

Sechrest, L. "Roots: Back to Our First Generations." Evaluation Practice, 1992, 13 (1), 1–7.

Van Maanen, J. Tales of the Field: On Writing Ethnography. Chicago: University of Chicago Press, 1988.

Yin, R. K. "Looking at Upside-Down Faces." Journal of Experimental Psychology, 1969, 81, 141–145.

Yin, R. K. "Face Recognition: A Special Process?" Unpublished doctoral dissertation, Department of Brain and Cognitive Sciences, Massachusetts Institute of Technology, 1970a.

Yin, R. K. "Face Recognition by Brain-Injured Patients: A Dissociable Ability?" Neuropsychologia, 1970b, 8, 395–402.

Yin, R. K. "Face Perception: A Review of Experiments with Infants, Normal Adults, and Brain-Injured Persons." In R. Held, H. W. Leibowitz, and H. L. Teuber (eds.), Handbook of Sensory Physiology. Vol. 8: Perception. New York: Springer-Verlag, 1978.

Yin, R. K. Case Study Research: Design and Methods. (Rev. ed.) Newbury Park, Calif.: Sage, 1989.

ROBERT K. YIN is president of COSMOS Corporation, a social science think tank in Washington, D.C.

The argument that the qualitative and quantitative paradigms are incompatible is not convincing. An enduring and beneficial partnership between qualitative and quantitative researchers is possible.

Qualitative and Quantitative Inquiries Are Not Incompatible: A Call for a New Partnership

Charles S. Reichardt, Sharon F. Rallis

Partners must have similar values if their partnerships are to endure. Of course, partners can be different. After all, opposites do attract. But for a relationship to work over an extended period of time, the partners usually must share basic ideologies. Incompatibility in fundamental values and beliefs is usually legitimate grounds, both legally and emotionally, for divorce.

Certainly, there are substantial differences between the qualitative and quantitative research traditions. The question is whether the qualitative and quantitative paradigms have enough similarities in fundamental values, in spite of their other differences, to form an enduring partnership. There are many who would answer negatively. In evaluation, perhaps the most widely cited proponents of incompatibility are Guba and Lincoln (1989; Guba, 1990; Lincoln, 1990), but there are others as well, including Heap (1992) and Smith and Heshusius (1986). Lincoln (1990, p. 81) stated her beliefs about incompatibility forthrightly: "The immediate realization is that accommodation between paradigms is impossible. The rules for action, for process, for discourse, for what is considered knowledge and truth, are so vastly different that, although procedurally we may appear to be undertaking the same search, in fact, we are led to vastly diverse, disparate, distinctive, and typically antithetical ends." In contrast, we believe that a meaningful and enduring partnership between qualitative and quantitative researchers based on shared fundamental values is both possible and desirable, a stance that we believe is held by the other authors in the present volume (also see Howe, 1988; Reichardt and Cook, 1979).

NEW DIRECTIONS FOR PROGRAM EVALUATION, no. 61, Spring 1994 © Jossey-Bass Publishers

In this chapter, we present our case for compatibility in two parts. In the first part, we examine presumed differences that incompatibilists believe force the paradigms apart. We argue that the incompatibilists' descriptions of these differences are inaccurate, and, as a result, we find their evidence for incompatibility unconvincing. In the second part, we describe shared fundamental values that are often overlooked by incompatibilists.

Logical Positivism Versus Postpositivism

Different writers use different names to refer to the qualitative and quantitative paradigms. Positivist is one of the names sometimes used to describe the quantitative paradigm. Part of the belief in the incompatibility of the qualitative and quantitative paradigms may arise because of a confusion over the meaning of this label. Specifically, the positivist label for the quantitative paradigm may blur the distinction between logical positivism and postpositivism. This blurring helps perpetuate the myth that logical positivism rather than postpositivism characterizes contemporary quantitative inquiry.

Logical positivism was discredited shortly after World War II and has since been abandoned (Phillips, 1990). The replacement for logical positivism was labeled postpositivism because it followed in time, not because it was similar philosophically. Some of the landmark works in postpositivism appeared in the late 1950s, including Popper ([1935] 1959) and Hanson (1958) (Phillips, 1987, 1990). By the 1960s and 1970s, the tenets of postpositivism were widely and unmistakably being integrated into the thinking of quantitative researchers in the social sciences. For example, Campbell and Stanley (1963, 1966) were unabashedly postpositivist and produced probably the single most influential work in quantitative evaluation during the late 1960s and throughout the 1970s, when the modern era of program evaluation was born in conjunction with Lyndon Johnson's Great Society programs. Cook and Campbell (1979) also reverently embraced postpositivism (also see Cook, 1983, 1985; and Campbell, 1974). And Cook and Campbell (1979) has probably been the most widely cited and influential reference in quantitative evaluation for the last fifteen years, becoming the new testament to Campbell and Stanley's (1966) old testament. Phillips (1987, 1990) and Garrison (1986) have thoroughly described some of the central postpositivist beliefs that characterize current thinking in the social sciences. Several of these beliefs are addressed below.

Theory-Ladenness of Facts

If we were told that a particular person was mentally ill, we might make sense of his or her behavior differently from what we would do if we were told the same person was an absent-minded professor (for example, see Rosenhan, 1973). Attributing this insight to Hanson (1958), Phillips (1987, p. 40) expressed the general principle as follows: "The theory, hypothesis, framework, or background knowledge held by an investigator can strongly influence what is observed." This principle is called the "theory-ladenness of facts."

This principle is a well-accepted belief in postpositivist and quantitative science (Garrison, 1986; Phillips, 1987, 1990; Campbell, 1974). For example, Cook and Campbell (1979, p. 24) explicitly stated that "we share the post-positivists' belief that observations are theory-laden." And it is noteworthy that evidence often cited in support of the theory-ladenness of facts is drawn from quantitative psychology (Phillips, 1987; Bruner and Potter, 1964).

Guba and Lincoln's (1989) thesis of incompatibility between the paradigms is based, in part, on the argument that the theory-ladenness of facts is a tenet of the qualitative paradigm but not of the quantitative paradigm (Guba and Lincoln, 1989, pp. 63, 105; Guba, 1990, p. 25). In contrast, we believe that the paradigms share the fundamental belief in the theory-ladenness of facts so that this is not a source of incompatibility.

Fallibility of Knowledge

Postpositivism is predicated on the notion that knowledge is fallible. Phillips (1990, p. 32) noted that this postpositivist view of knowledge "fits comfortably with what every experienced action researcher and evaluator of social programs has come to understand about his or her own work; these are, par excellence, fields of 'the believable,' of building the 'good case,' but where even the best of cases can be challenged or reanalyzed or reinterpreted. Nothing is more suspicious in the field of evaluation than a report that is presented with the implication that it has the status of 'holy writ.' " One of the founding fathers of postpositivism made the same point even more concisely: "We do not know: we can only guess" (Popper, [1935] 1959, p. 278). Campbell and Stanley (1966, p. 35) also supported the same view: "The results of an experiment 'probe' but do not 'prove' a theory. An adequate hypothesis is one that has repeatedly survived such probing—but it may always be displaced by a new probe." Cook and Campbell (1979, p. 22) subscribed to this position as follows: "It is our inescapable predicament that we cannot prove a theory or other causal proposition."

Guba and Lincoln's (1989) thesis of incompatibility between the paradigms is also based, in part, on presumed differences in beliefs about the fallibility of knowledge. They argued that the qualitative paradigm understands that knowledge is "subject to continuous refinement, revision, and, if necessary, replacement" (1979, p. 104). But they also argued that the quantitative paradigm holds to the belief that knowledge is "definitive and enduring" and that "truth is absolute" (pp. 103–104). In contrast, we believe that the paradigms share the belief in the fallibility of knowledge so that this is not a source of incompatibility.

Underdetermination of Theory by Fact

The principle of the underdetermination of theory by fact states that any given set of data can always be explained by many different theories. In support of their incompatibility thesis, Guba and Lincoln (1989, pp. 63–64; Guba, 1990, p. 25) argued that this principle is accepted by the qualitative paradigm but not by the quantitative paradigm.

In contrast, we believe that the quantitative paradigm accepts the principle of the underdetermination of theory by fact just as devoutly as the qualitative paradigm. For example, Campbell and Stanley (1966, p. 36) forthrightly noted that "at any stage of accumulation of evidence, even for the most advanced science, there are numerous possible theories compatible with the data." Similarly, Cook and Campbell (1979, p. 22) noted that no matter how much data are collected ("by expanding as much as we can the number, range, and precision of confirmed predictions"), and no matter how many rival hypotheses are ruled out, the number of rival hypotheses "still remains in some sense infinite." Both Phillips (1990, p. 35) and Garrison (1986, p. 14) also described the principle of the underdetermination of theory by fact as a central tenet of postpositivist philosophy.

Value-Ladenness of Inquiry

A researcher's values enter into research in many ways. The choice of a question to investigate, a theoretical stance to guide the investigation, and a set of results to report are all shaped by the investigator's values. The principle that research is influenced by values is called the "value-ladenness of inquiry."

In support of their belief in incompatibility, Guba and Lincoln (1989, p. 105; Guba, 1990, p. 25) argued that the value-ladenness of inquiry is antithetical to quantitative inquiry but is central to the qualitative paradigm. In contrast, we do not believe that the value-ladenness of inquiry is antithetical to the quantitative paradigm but rather is accepted by many quantitative researchers. For example, Guba and Lincoln (1989, p. 101) provided six references to the work of "individuals who do not see themselves outside the pale of the conventional [that is, quantitative] paradigm" and who accept the principle of the value-ladenness of inquiry.

Nature of Reality

According to Guba and Lincoln (1989, p. 12), the qualitative paradigm believes that "reality . . . is constructed by people" while the quantitative paradigm does not. This principle of the construction of reality can be given a variety of different meanings. One interpretation is that one's understanding of reality is constructed. In this form, the belief in the construction of reality is shared by most qualitative and quantitative researchers. A second interpretation is that people's actions can influence the world so as to shape it in the ways they want (or sometimes do not want). This belief is also shared by most qualitative and quantitative researchers. Another interpretation is that people are in complete control of physical reality, able, for example, to change lead to gold by whim. This belief is not accepted by most quantitative researchers, but neither is it accepted by most qualitative researchers.

Guba and Lincoln (1989, pp. 12–13; emphasis in original) also asserted that qualitative researchers believe that "realities are not objectively 'out there'" and that "there is no reality except that created by people." If this assumption means that reality influences people only via their perceptions or sensations, this view is shared by quantitative researchers. On the other hand, if this statement is meant to imply that there are no external referents for people's understanding of reality, this is likely to be a source of severe incompatibility between the paradigms, because quantitative researchers tend to hold to a "realist" assumption about nature. However, a belief that there are no external referents for one's understandings would also be incompatible with the practice of program evaluation, for there would be no programs to evaluate. In any case, we believe that qualitative researchers generally share a realist perspective along with quantitative researchers.

Other Shared Ideologies

Evaluators share a commitment to understanding and improving the human condition. Evaluators believe that they can provide usable knowledge about social problems and about strategies to address them. These commitments and values transcend differences between qualitative and quantitative inquiries and in some sense serve to unite us. That is, while our different epistemologies may part us, our shared ideologies partner us.

We may never agree on the causes of homelessness, or even on the best way to study homelessness, but we all agree that homelessness is an undesirable condition and that society should strive to alleviate it. We also agree that a deeper understanding of homelessness and its context is likely to be required if society is to solve this problem. We may never agree how best to capture what and how a student learns, but we share the goal of improving student learning and improving our understanding of learning in and out of the classroom.

As evaluators, we seek to inform. We recognize the importance of producing knowledge, whether policymakers and practitioners use it directly to inform their decisions or whether it is added to an accumulating pool of knowledge that ultimately shapes the decisions made by policymakers and practitioners. While we may disagree on the most usable forms in which to obtain and present knowledge, we agree that our goal is to package it so that it can be shared and used.

We agree that the world is complex and stratified, and often difficult to understand. And we agree on the need for rigor, conscientiousness, and critiques as we undertake the difficult task of creating knowledge.

Conclusion

According to the American Psychological Association Task Force on Psychology and Education (McCombs, 1991), one of the twelve principles of learning is that working with others of different styles and perspectives enhances learning. Can the differences in style and perspective between qualitative and quantitative inquiry enhance learning? Or are the differences so great that they preclude the possibility of working together?

Some qualitative and quantitative researchers may hold views that are so disparate that they are incompatible. But we do not believe that the views of the majority of qualitative and quantitative researchers are of this nature. Quite the contrary, many fundamental values are shared by the qualitative and quantitative research traditions, and the differences that exist can be used both to enlighten each other and to better serve our clients. It is thus to our and our clients' benefit to begin the hard work that is required to develop and maintain an enduring and rewarding partnership.

References

Bruner, J. S., and Potter, M. C. "Interference in Visual Recognition." Science, 1964, 144, 424–425.

Campbell, D. T. "Evolutionary Epistemology." In P. A. Schilpp (ed.), The Library of Living Philosophers. Vol. 14: The Philosophy of Karl Popper. La Salle, Ill.: Open Court, 1974.

Campbell, D. T., and Stanley, J. C. "Experimental and Quasi-Experimental Designs for Research on Teaching." In N. L. Gage (ed.), Handbook of Research on Teaching. Skokie, Ill.: Rand McNally, 1963.

Campbell, D. T., and Stanley, J. C. Experimental and Quasi-Experimental Designs for Research. Skokie, Ill.: Rand McNally, 1966.

Cook, T. D. "Quasi-Experimentation: Its Ontology, Epistemology, and Methodology." In G. Morgan (ed.), Beyond Method: Strategies for Social Research. Newbury Park, Calif.: Sage, 1983.

Cook, T. D. "Postpositivist Critical Multiplism." In R. L. Shotland and M. M. Mark (eds.), Social Science and Social Policy. Newbury Park, Calif.: Sage, 1985.

Cook, T. D., and Campbell, D. T. Quasi-Experimentation: Design and Analysis Issues for Field Settings. Skokie, Ill.: Rand McNally, 1979.

Garrison, J. W. "Some Principles of Postpositivistic Philosophy of Science." Educational Researcher, 1986, 15, 12–18.

Guba, E. G. "The Alternative Paradigm Dialog." In E. G. Guba (ed.), The Paradigm Dialog. Newbury Park, Calif.: Sage, 1990.

Guba, E. G., and Lincoln, Y. S. Fourth-Generation Evaluation. Newbury Park, Calif.: Sage, 1989.

Hanson, N. R. Patterns of Discovery: An Inquiry into the Conceptual Foundations of Science. Cambridge, England: Cambridge University Press, 1958.

Heap, J. L. "Ethnomethodology and the Possibility of a Metaperspective on Literacy Research." In R. Beach, J. L. Green, M. L. Kamil, and T. Shanahan (eds.), Multidisciplinary Perspectives on Literacy Research. Urbana, Ill.: National Council of Teachers of English, 1992.

Howe, K. R. "Against the Quantitative-Qualitative Incompatibility Thesis, or Dogmas Die Hard." Educational Researcher, 1988, 17 (8), 10–16.

Lincoln, Y. S. "The Making of a Constructivist: A Remembrance of Transformations Past." In E. G. Guba (ed.), The Paradigm Dialog. Newbury Park, Calif.: Sage, 1990.

McCombs, B. L. Learning-Centered Psychological Principles: Guidelines for School Redesign and Reform. Washington, D.C.: American Psychological Association, 1991.

Phillips, D. C. "On What Scientists Know, and How They Know It." In W. R. Shadish, Jr., and C. S. Reichardt (eds.), Evaluation Studies Review Annual. Vol. 12. Newbury Park, Calif.: Sage, 1987.

Phillips, D. C. "Postpositivist Science: Myths and Realities." In E. G. Guba (ed.), The Paradigm Dialog. Newbury Park, Calif.: Sage, 1990.

Popper, K. R. The Logic of Scientific Discovery. New York: Basic Books, 1959. (Originally published 1935.)

Reichardt, C. S., and Cook, T. D. "Beyond Qualitative Versus Quantitative Methods." In T. D. Cook and C. S. Reichardt (eds.), Qualitative and Quantitative Methods in Evaluation Research. Newbury Park, Calif.: Sage, 1979.

Rosenhan, D. L. "On Being Sane in Insane Places." Science, 1973, 179, 250–258.

Smith, J. K., and Heshusius, L. "Closing Down the Conversation: The End of the Quantitative-Qualitative Debate Among Educational Inquirers." Educational Researcher, 1986, 15 (1), 4–12.

CHARLES S. REICHARDT is professor of psychology at the University of Denver.

SHARON F. RALLIS is coordinator of the Designing Schools for Enhanced Learning Program of the Regional Laboratory for Educational Improvement of the Northeast and Islands, Andover, Massachusetts.

INDEX

Ordering Information

NEW DIRECTIONS FOR PROGRAM EVALUATION is a series of paperback books that presents the latest techniques and procedures for conducting useful evaluation studies of all types of programs. Books in the series are published quarterly in Spring, Summer, Fall, and Winter and are available for purchase by subscription as well as by single copy.

SUBSCRIPTIONS for 1994 cost $54.00 for individuals (a savings of 34 percent over single-copy prices) and $75.00 for institutions, agencies, and libraries. Please do not send institutional checks for personal subscriptions. Standing orders are accepted.

SINGLE COPIES cost $17.95 when payment accompanies order. (California, New Jersey, New York, and Washington, D.C., residents please include appropriate sales tax.) Billed orders will be charged postage and handling.

DISCOUNTS FOR QUANTITY ORDERS are available. Please write to the address below for information.

ALL ORDERS must include either the name of an individual or an official purchase order number. Please submit your order as follows:
   Subscriptions: specify series and year subscription is to begin
   Single copies: include individual title code (such as PE59)

MAIL ALL ORDERS TO:
   Jossey-Bass Publishers
   350 Sansome Street
   San Francisco, California 94104-1342

FOR SINGLE-COPY SALES OUTSIDE OF THE UNITED STATES, CONTACT:
   Maxwell Macmillan International Publishing Group
   866 Third Avenue
   New York, New York 10022-6221

FOR SUBSCRIPTION SALES OUTSIDE OF THE UNITED STATES, CONTACT:
   any international subscription agency or Jossey-Bass directly.

OTHER TITLES AVAILABLE IN THE
NEW DIRECTIONS FOR PROGRAM EVALUATION SERIES
William R. Shadish, Editor-in-Chief